BEFORE YOU BEGIN...

Take a moment and breathe. Place your hand over your chest area, near your heart. Breathe slowly into the area for about a minute, focusing on a sense of ease entering your mind and body.

-

-

-

-

-

The simple exercise you were just introduced to is designed to help create a physiological heart brain connection that has been shown to improve memory, learning, problem-solving and discernment.

"What just happened?"

Blue Hand Books

Greenfield, Massachusetts

Creative Non-Fiction | Native America Poetry, Prophecy, Military and Illustrated History

© 02021 WHAT JUST HAPPENED? (code: **Whiskey Juliet Hotel**)

Cover Photo: Anecia Tretikoff... Marmot in Alaska (2020)

Other Photos by author, Death to Stock Photo/Microsoft Clip Art (including Military Industrial Complex) and Pinterest. Quotes sourced.

PUBLISHER: Blue Hand Books, 25 Keegan Lane, Suite 8c, GREENFIELD, MASSACHUSETTS 01301

WEBSITE: www.bluehandbooks.org

ISBN: 978-057886725-0

First Edition

BOOK SERIES: It's a MIRACLE We've Survived this Far

Book 1: Mental Midgets | Musqonocihte

5 stars Emotional. Truthful. Intensely absorbing. Eloquent.

Reviewed November 29, 2018: You get such an emotional response from each page. Your mind shouts, "Yes, This is truth." As you read. Some passages leave you bleeding and stunned. Others have you shaking your head. These collections and musings are quite stirring. The truth can be quite ugly.—Janice L Roper

Pretty sure the wife spittin' FIRE just changed my life.
—Herbism (look for them throughout the book)

BLUE INDIANS COLLECTIVE
NATIVE AMERICAN AUTHORS

How do I read this book?

Do what I do. First, Read: Start to Finish. Close book. Take a nap. Later open at any page and spend three minutes making a mini-movie in your mind about all your new ideas. Next week: Randomly open book and Scribble Doodle on any page. Add notes, code or symbols, if you feel like it. I make up new hobo code (see below)

Last thing: HAVE FUN! V

GOOD MORNING! Good Afternoon. Good Evening y'all.

A	ALPHA	.—
B	BRAVO	—...
C	CHARLIE	—.—.
D	DELTA	—..
E	ECHO	.
F	FOXTROT	..—.
G	GOLF	——.
H	HOTEL	....
I	INDIA	..
J	JULIET	.———
K	KILO	—.—
L	LIMA	.—..
M	MIKE	——
N	NOVEMBER	—.
O	OSCAR	———
P	PAPA	.——.
Q	QUEBEC	——.—
R	ROMEO	.—.
S	SIERRA	...
T	TANGO	—
U	UNIFORM	..—
V	VICTOR	...—
W	WISKEY	.——
X	XRAY	—..—
Y	YANKEE	—.——
Z	ZULU	——..

Pray tell... WHAT JUST HAPPENED? (eh... that's the book title) I do say this every single day.

You do, too, maybe?

The book title (**Whiskey Juliet Hotel**) is not exactly code. But I do use code. Why? **We see what they WANT us to see and then they TELL us what we see** (this is not the book subtitle but it could be).

Code is usually disguised, hidden. (Q and followers ANON and others use it openly.) Code is not always in words but hand gestures, images, memes, ideas.

About seeing what they want us to see? I've made other plans for us.

TANGO ROMEO UNIFORM ECHO?

True. I will prove it to you. Just wait.

Who are **they**? Some dastardly slippery tongue fellows. Rogues? Deep State? Your neighbor? Your president? Your bad uncle?

(CODE GRAPHIC Microsoft Clipart)

SOME NIGHTS
I FEEL SO CLOSE
TO FIGURING IT
OUT

SO CLOSE TO SOME
EPIPHANY THAT
WILL MAKE ALL OF
THIS SUFFERING
MAKE SENSE

Anyone else wrapped up in a blanket watching TV or YouTube while they do their dirty rotten tricks in the back yard while we're glued to our screens in the front room? (Left: Quote: Unknown)

:: Hotel Echo Lima Papa ::

Anyone who can discern (think, ponder, daydream) to any degree understands everything and everyone is inter-connected. Yes: you, me, stardust, the mountains, the grizzly bears, the great lakes, the glaciers, the bees, and so on.

All us dots <u>connect </u>to one another. (We're webbed very tightly together.)

At this age, I *think* I know a little more about how things work IRL (in real life). (I'm an elder.) With this new collection I've compiled... it will help me (and you and us) to be coherent and calm and put things in perspective. (The rogue fellows do love to create big chaotic gusts of confusion so we *think* we can't think.)

Wicked smart to keep us "occupied" with bullsh*t and ballgames and bargains for so long!

Their spell broken by a virus? Maybe so. Their fire was extinguished. Movie titans in hollyweird lost the spark and any magic they had simply pooped out.

"Always thought being a writer would be one of the most useless things you could be in a zombie apocalypse, but it turns out arts and culture and storytelling is what helps us get through. Along with science, doctors, nurses, delivery people, farm workers and supermarket cashiers."—Author **Lauren Beukes**

TANGO ROMEO UNIFORM ECHO?

Distraction ALWAYS works, I was told by my Northern Cheyenne friend Steve Little Coyote in Seattle in the 90s....
Especially when you see Barbie Dolls on the TV news. (Jot that down for future reference.) (Watch out, someone is definitely distracting us.) (Oh and whenever you see British royals on American TV making headlines.)

I say to myself, "Self, the system ain't broke, it was built this way." Let that sink in. Obviously I write down something— just when I think I have figured out what is going on, then I'm smacked upside the head and find even more for this book.

Like this:

OCCULTIST?
US president Donald Trump is more magician than politician. Reality is whatever he says it is. He casts a spell on supporters with exclamations and incantations, outrageous and outraged tweets and speeches, flights of fancy rather than fact. Trump isn't hemmed in by pesky old-times notions, like rules. He does and says what he wants when he wants, acknowledging only what suits him. In this sense, the US president resembles the early 20th century occultist Aleister Crowley.
(READ: https://qz.com/1364997/the-startling-parallels-between-donald-trump-and-occultist-aleister-crowley/)

Yes, I am pretty sure that if I knew everything going on, I'd hate it.

Antediluvian Masonry And The Seven Sacred Sciences

https://decodingsatan.blogspot.com/2016/10/antediluvian-masonry-and-seven-sacred.html

Seven Sacred Sciences" in the English Ordinal system equals 192. Seven Sacred Sciences" in the English Sumerian system equals 1152. Seven Sacred Sciences" in the English Gematria system equals 1038. Seven Sacred Sciences" in the Greek Beta Code system equals 1420.

What are the seven Sacred Sciences? | Yahoo Answers

https://answers.yahoo.com/question/index?qid=20070418042926AAasj48

What are the seven Sacred Sciences? In a mural on the wall of the Spanish Chapel of Santa Maria Novella, beneath the depiction of Thomas Aquinas, are figures representing the Liberal Arts and the Sacred Sciences...what exactly are they?

Here's a good example: Grammar, Rhetoric, Logic, Astronomy, Arithmetic, Geometry and Music—each and every one are made up, all a figment of someone's imagination or a weapon or a guess. Not advanced knowledge or some magical cosmic intelligence. No. They are just called the Seven Sacred Sciences. Roman/British, probably. Sacred, no way. No, really, no way! Stop and think about this...primitive music exists in different harmonics or hertz (Hz.) But someone stopped it and altered it! WHY? I have been called hard-headed in the past (and worse) but processing this took me a very long time... now you will be processing this a long time, too.

Maybe that is what Tesla meant when he said if you understood the power of 3-6-9, you'd have the key to the universe... yikes! (keep reading...)

You may not realize how much America's Military Industrial Complex has built and the immense arsenal Americans paid for. You'll see for yourself in Section 3.

(Military: Microsoft clipart)

Sap and insect "honeydew" from the Tamarisk tree is often referred to as MANNA. The Ark of the Covenant was a wooden chest, with contents: a pot, some manna, and Aaron's rod. Manna is called a Gift from On High. It rains from the Heavens.

Time and Timing

12.12.2020
12.21.2020

Will the simulation end? No.

12.12.21
12.21.21

Will the simulation end? No.

Time is an illusion. Follow the earthquakes. Volcanos are coming.

Music altered?

I did a little digging and found out **Solfeggio Frequencies** make up the ancient 6-tone scale thought to have been used in sacred music, including the well-known Gregorian Chants. The special tones were believed to impart spiritual blessings when sung in harmony. Each Solfeggio tone is comprised of a frequency required to balance your energy and keep your body, mind and spirit in perfect harmony.

Someone wrote: The Solfeggio frequencies were **lost** because throughout history different tuning applications have been used. (Uh-hum, sure)

We know that Nikola Tesla, the great genius and father of electromagnetic engineering, had once said, "If you only knew the magnificence of the 3, 6 and 9, then you would hold a key to the universe." The 3, 6, and 9 are the fundamental root vibrations of the Solfeggio frequencies.

And Albert Einstein figured out that: "Concerning matter, we have been all wrong. What we have called matter is energy, whose vibration has been so lowered as to be perceptible to the senses. There is no matter." All matter beings vibrate at specific rates and everything has its own melody. The musical nature of nuclear matter from atoms to galaxies is now finally being recognized by science.

Why these frequencies are so powerful? They can literally bring you back to the original tones of the heavenly spheres and put your body into a balanced resonance.

Solfeggio music is the key to the Universe.

IMAGE: https://drprem.com/wellness/wp-content/uploads/sites/7/2020/02/Solfeggio-frequencies.jpg

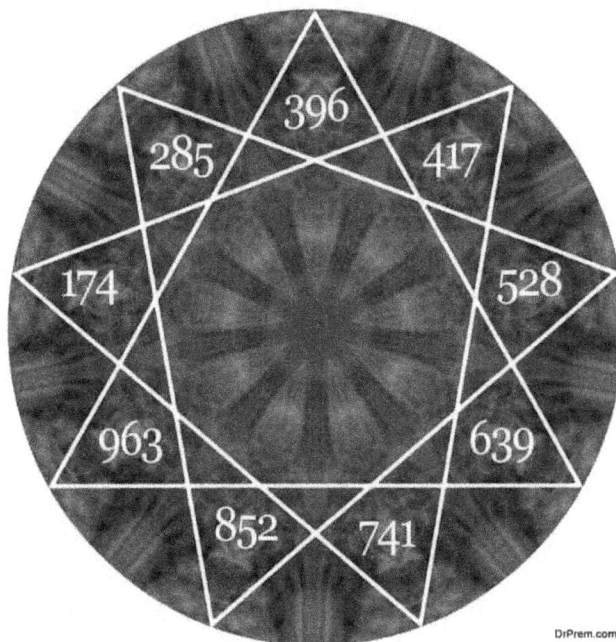

I also read that Tesla described his discovery and invention of the mechanical oscillator that sent vibrations through the body at various frequencies as **his greatest contribution to human well-being**, a bold statement for an inventor on the level of Nikola Tesla. WOW!

Throughout the rest of his life, he would use his oscillation machine (BELOW) to treat people with a wide variety of health problems—from constipation to cardiovascular disease, injuries and infections, sleep disorders, and hormonal imbalances.

But exactly what was it that he had discovered?
As Tesla himself said:
"If you want to find the secrets of the universe, think in terms of energy, frequency and vibration."

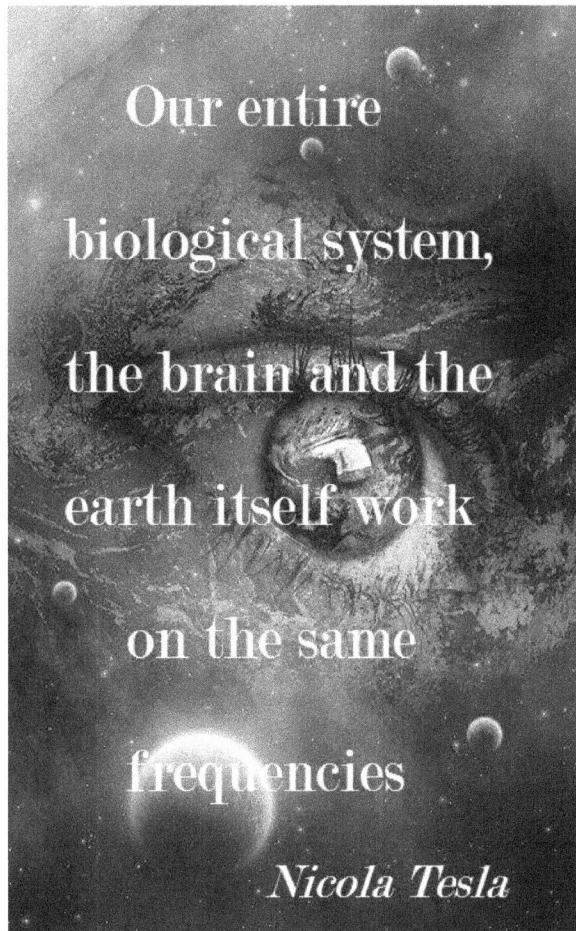

Our entire biological system, the brain and the earth itself work on the same frequencies

Nicola Tesla

VISIT:
https://teslauniverse.com

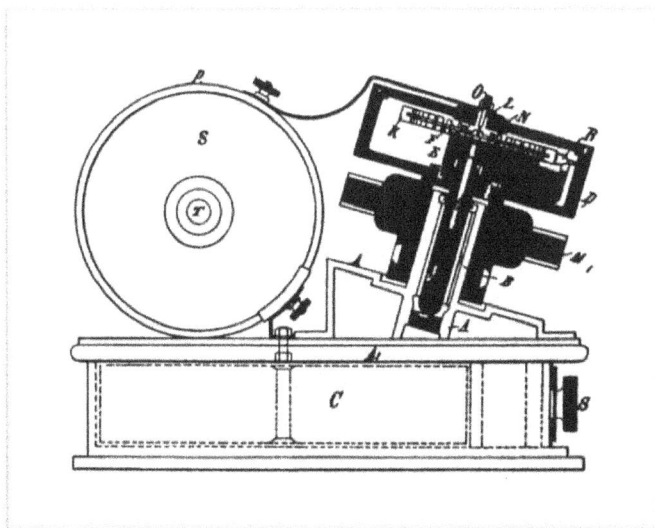

> **....WE DON'T THINK LIKE HUMAN BEINGS ANYMORE, WE DON'T IDENTIFY AS HUMAN BEINGS. WE ARE CITIZENS OR REPUBLICANS OR DEMOCRATS OR LIBERALS OR LEFTISTS OR INDIANS OR WOMEN OR MEN OR VICTIMS; WE'RE EVERYTHING BUT A HUMAN BEING.**
> **-JOHN TRUDELL**

A reason to be optimistic?

*"This planned future, however, is NOT preordained. Totalitarian transhumanism is not a foregone conclusion. Trudell's remedy? Change our perception of reality through active non-cooperation. Manifest in our hearts, minds, and actions the world **we** desire. Where they engineer disconnect, RECONNECT with intention; not only with one another, but with ALL our relations and the land and the spiritual beings that exist beyond our senses. We must synchronize to change the vibrational reality, and that power exists within us as children of the earth."* — **Journalist Makia Freeman**

See more in Section 4.

Watch: Coded Bias on Netflix. I did! OMG!

The alternative to merging with the AI machine (artificial intelligence) is to become more fully human, super natural, intuitive, psychic, and magical. With love and as a united humanity we can heal the earth. —SUNBOW, superbly good online comment

...and here I'm thinking that A.I. was about stirring up division...no, no, it's worse. It's perverting the history of who we are, too! The end of humanity (AGAIN)? If Atlantis was destroyed by technology, we could be, too.

Top AI companies in 2020

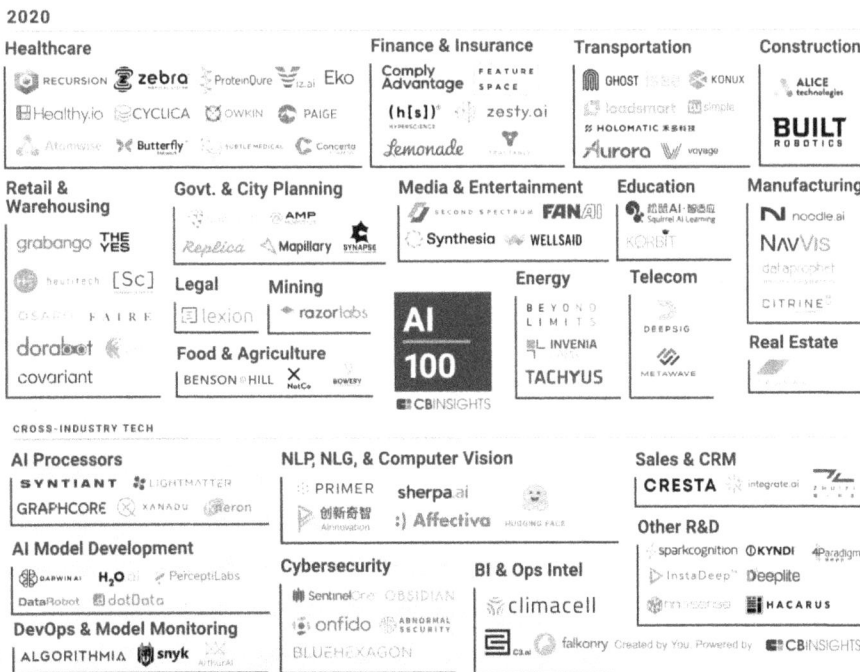

IMAGE: https://www.cbinsights.com/research/report/artificial-intelligence-top-startups/

LOOK UP! My photo: Vermont Sky Writing

What I've been thinking since the last book

—A WHOLE LOT, just in case!

...and about ~~SEVEN~~ EIGHT BILLION SOULS and counting.

Since 2015/6, we got hit with a tsunami of gaslighting* which will require more than a paragraph or two to explain... some are calling this 1996-2021 timeline THE BIG LIE. (That is gaslighting, too, while certainly confusing us.)

DICE: Quote: Charles Bukowski (1920-1944)

roll the dice

if you're going to try, go all the way.
otherwise, don't even start.

*gaslighting:

Unscrupulous leaders have been using a technique pioneered by Adolf Hitler of discovering what people wish is true or fear is true, then telling them that it IS true. You destroy freedom by getting people to believe lies, and the sudden and dramatic increase in the depth of communication caused by the internet has enabled liars to temporarily gain a great deal of power.

The military industrial complex or "Corporation" in America doesn't make mistakes... it makes monster mistakes. (see Section 3) We are constantly and carefully being manipulated with a brain massage every. single. day.

We haven't been steering the boat... not for a long time... watching the military psy-op called TV. (Herb-ism)

THE TELEVISION WILL NOT BE REVOLUTIONIZED... (and no, the revolution will not be televised)

Let's think about our twice-impeached former President who apparently never read state department daily briefs, or national security updates, or worked a day in his life as a politician prior, or paid any heed to disasters unless it affected his holdings and profits, etc.

Maybe the military was relieved this dope didn't read? They had him surveilled, of course. All those secret Putin meeting were taped for sure. Every phone call was monitored and taped for future...errr... blackmail?

I don't even want to imagine what son-in-law JARED will do with all that intelligence (gathered globally) that **HE** read daily. Smacks of intrigue, right? More blackmail? Did he make copies? Did the military plant some fake stuff to see if Jared will sell it? (It's just a hunch.)

Wait, what? The Donald doesn't read? How inept was he?

Nope, #45 wanted crowds of clappers (he even paid for clappers) ...he lived for large rallies, money and applause. (I wrote an op-ed for a newspaper and you will read it in this book: **A very bad breakup**)

What did #45 do all day? Watched TELEVISION mostly, talked to friends, Fox News anchors, oh, and he golfed.

But he did cause an uproar with #STOPTHESTEAL on Jan. 6, 2021. Now called a SEIGE ON THE CAPITOL. During his SAVE AMERICA MARCH, people were not saved but killed—and that was not good news. The Big Lie, pushed hard by Trump and his supporters, was that Trump had won the 2020 election and it had been stolen by the Democrats. Although this was entirely discredited in more than 60 lawsuits, the Big Lie inspired Trump supporters to rally to defend their president and, they thought, their country. (A new 2021 Reuters/Ipsos found that six in ten Republicans believe this Big Lie.)

Trump was very easy to manipulate. And "His People" were, too. (Herb-ism)

"The devil is a saint compared to Donald Trump." –Former Trump Advisor on TV

**

Wake up Wilbur! Way back in July 2019

A news report revealed that **Wilbur Ross**, President Donald Trump's beleaguered commerce secretary, is so bad at his **job** that he often falls asleep while working. The Commerce Department is operating disastrously, according to a report from Politico that also claims that Secretary Wilbur Ross finds it impossible to stay awake in meetings. The 81-year-old is rarely seen at the department, according to Politico's sources. "He's sort of seen as kind of irrelevant," said one unnamed source. "The morale is very low there because there's not a lot of confidence in the secretary... He's not respected in the building." He also doesn't hold routine meetings due to a reported lack of stamina, with one source saying: "There's a small window where he's able to focus and pay attention and not fall asleep."

"What just happened?" Waking Wilbur asked.

Whiskey Juliet Hotel: WHAT JUST HAPPENED?

Trump was elected in 2016 and TV networks hit a **massive** new payload of viewers and the highest ratings—ever? BIG MEDIA lusted for this. They LOVED this. They needed him BIGLY to be reelected in 2020. (Oh darn, he lost.) Now #45 is talking about running for President again in 2024? Smell money?

(My TV Screenshot)

Tanking TV ratings since Trump lost (MSM losing money too)

Change in U.S. Total Audience Watching Weekday Primetime Cable News for Week of 1/25 - 1/29 vs. 1/18 - 1/22

How to read: CNN average viewership across 1/25 through 1/29 was down by -43.69% in the 8pm hour among total viewers aged 2+ watching live or within 24 hours of airing

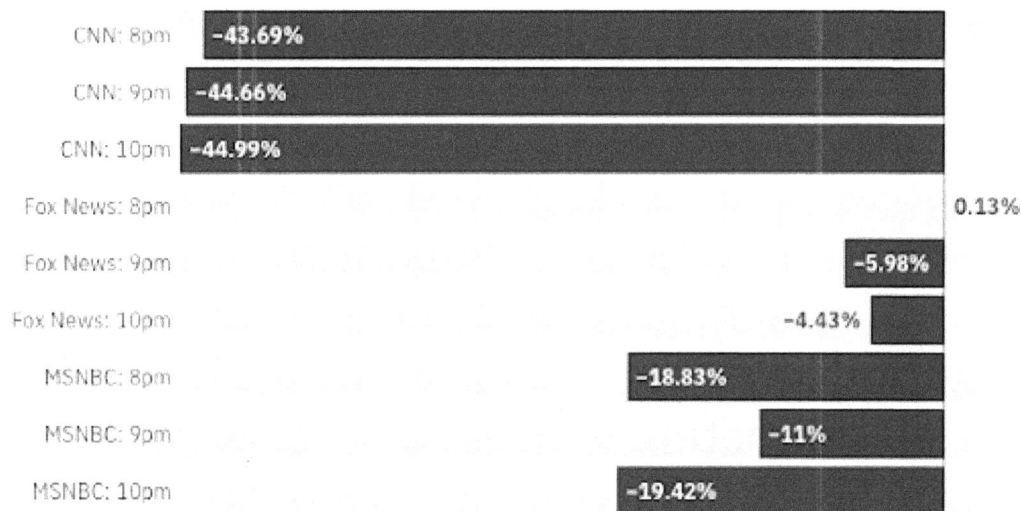

CNN: 8pm	-43.69%
CNN: 9pm	-44.66%
CNN: 10pm	-44.99%
Fox News: 8pm	0.13%
Fox News: 9pm	-5.98%
Fox News: 10pm	-4.43%
MSNBC: 8pm	-18.83%
MSNBC: 9pm	-11%
MSNBC: 10pm	-19.42%

Trump clearly belongs to a rapidly de-evolving species of feces-flinging Orangutan. —Mike Burch

**Shane Goldmacher at the *New York Times* broke a story in April 2021: in the closing days of the 2020 election season, the Trump campaign scammed supporters out of more than $122 million by tricking them into "recurring" donations. The campaign had to refund those donations after the election, and it apparently did so by using money raised after the election by asking for funds to challenge the election results. In effect, supporters unknowingly made a no-interest loan to the campaign.

The United States is a freak global outlier in its enrichment of the rich, its acceptance of poverty, its military spending, and it's shunning of basic human rights to housing, education, and healthcare. Why would anyone elect another same-old schmuck? Why is this even a question?—David Swanson, Writer, Dandelion Salad

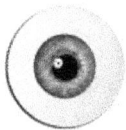

We could be collaborating with each other and with our ecosystem to create a beautiful, awesome, healthy world. Instead we're all competing with each other working meaningless jobs creating pieces of landfill which serve no purpose besides turning millionaires into billionaires.— Author Caitlin Johnstone, *Woke: A Field Guide for Utopia Preppers*.

Do you have TDS?

The accelerated downfall of the mainstream media (MSM) occurred since the election of Donald Trump. It's apparent that the MSM has caught TDS, or Trump Derangement Syndrome. I don't know what you feel or sense when you are watching the MSM, whether it's CNN, MSNBC who are obviously liberal networks or FOX News who is aligned with the Republicans party, it's almost like watching the Twilight Zone. Journalistic integrity has been absolutely flushed down the toilet. **—Timothy Alexander Guzman of Silent Crow News**

Funny Road Sign, Pinterest

Jake Tapper ✔ @jaketapper · 16h   ···

On the morning of January 6, Alexander said on Breitbart News Daily: "The president's ...in fighter mode and today will determine which Republicans are going to suffer his wrath going forward. ...I got a call last night from Kimberly Guilfoyle and none of us are stopping."

> **Olivia Little** @OliviaLittle · 19h
>
> SCOOP: "Stop The Steal" organizer bragged about a phone call with "people from the White House" weeks before the insurrection.
>
> In the same video, Ali Alexander also appeared to advocate for violence against lawmakers. mediamatters.org/january-6-insu...

◯ 217   ⟳ 3.2K   ♡ 6.8K   ⬆

(ah those crazy tweets)

Trump never wanted to *be* President.
Trump just wanted to be *called* President.
He only wanted the title, not the work or responsibility that came with it.
And as the death toll rises and the evidence of his inaction rises, it shows.

— TrumpsTaxes (@TrumpsTaxes) April 28, 2020

Donald Trump does not want to be in charge of any of this. He wants to play president on TV. He doesn't want responsibility for governance in a time of crisis, and in every way he can, he's refusing to do that job, and lashing out at those who ask him to do it.

— Ezra Klein (@ezraklein) April 29, 2020

A grown man tazed himself in the balls to death
A woman caring a "Don't tread on me" flag was trampled to death
The woman shot by police had just RTed a message about traitors getting the firing line
And my little fire-blackened soul is lit up with the joy of karmic poetry.

— ❧ Otto Lontra ❧ (@OttoLontra) January 8, 2021

BAGGY EYES

2016? 2017? 2018? 2019? 2020? 2021? I call them the YEARS OF BAGGY EYES. Did you notice all the bags??? There were scads of news anchors and politicians with saggy baggy eyes on air—a huge first in my recollection since TV hit our living rooms. Make-up can't fix those under eye bags... only sleep can.

MAYBE **no one** was sleeping well? (Sure, I have bags.)

Was it disbelief Trump won? The BIG LIE? Or was it 25,000 + documented lies? Or the average of 15 lies a day?

Why lie all the time? (go back and read gaslighting)

Are there still supporters of the past president?

Indeed, yes.

How do you persuade people to become followers and fanatics?

Look for marginalized, traumatized, vulnerable, poor, alienated (white) (male) teens to recruit. Kiddies need to be born into religious extremism, so it'll be super easy for them to be recruited online. Educate the shit out of them, and especially bore them with tainted history so they never open another book. Offer them identity, community, even purpose. Use TV and social media to reach out to them. Foment fear to get the violence to erupt and spew out of them. Create imaginary enemies? Ahhhh... that is so easy... these are reliably trusted Nazi-KKK recruitment tools.

A cartoon by Ted Littleford (above) https://www.tedlittleford.com/

Below: Graphic: Steal Like an Artist book, Austin Kleon)

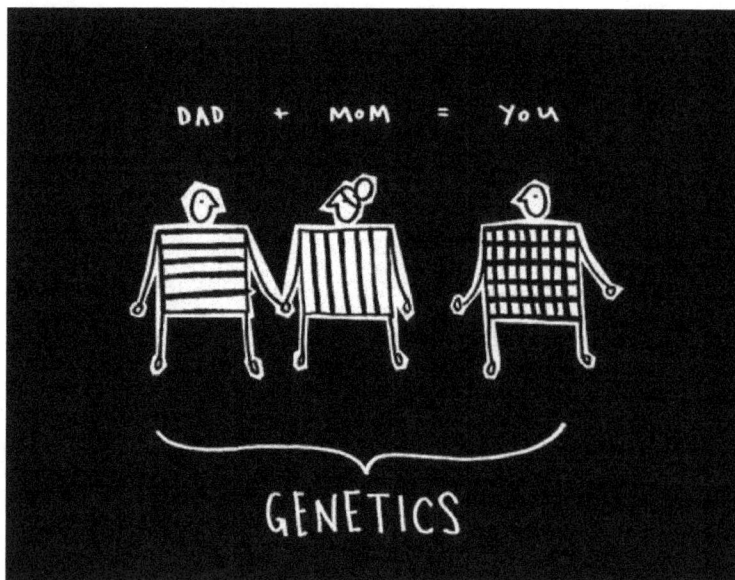

"I know what they fear now. They don't want us thinking."

John Trudell

GC

(Image: John Trudell, 1946-2019, www.johntrudell.com) Read Section 4.

Illusion Of Choice

There Are:

1,500 Newspapers

1,100 Magazines

9,000 Radio Stations

1,500 TV Stations

2,400 Publishers

Owned by 6 Corporations

& 272 Executives

That control 90 % of what 277 million Americans SEE, HEAR & READ

MINTPRESS NEWS

See what they want you to see? See? Image: Mint Press News

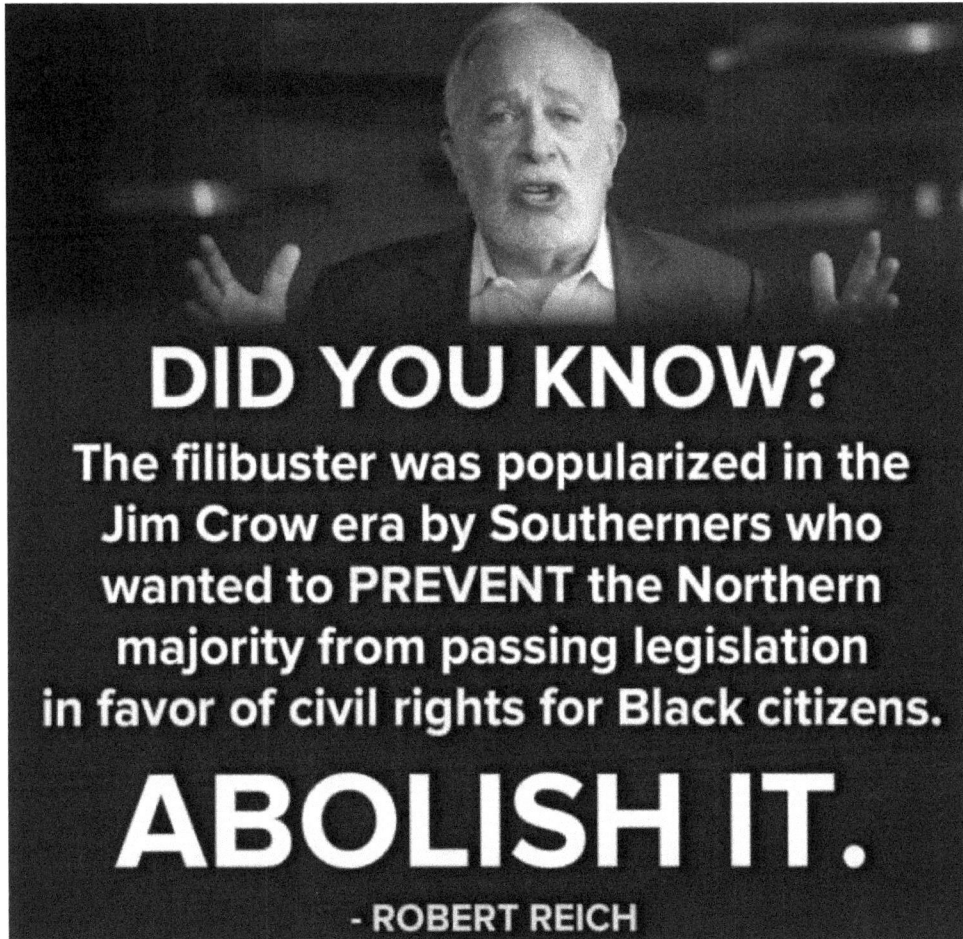

DID YOU KNOW?
The filibuster was popularized in the Jim Crow era by Southerners who wanted to PREVENT the Northern majority from passing legislation in favor of civil rights for Black citizens.
ABOLISH IT.
- ROBERT REICH

Unprecedented.

That is one word when you think of the past few years. We see Systemic Racism. Add a big dose of stress, fear-based trauma. Feeling disturbed yet?

Another word?

Stain.

America has been stained repeatedly.

Who says we can't criticize the government?

Are we so sure **everything** is a Conspiracy Theory? I think the cruelty we see in people like Trump has always been here... since the gunboats pulled up on Turtle Island. Trump was just a tool. ***Just like other presidents.*** The military industrial complex does this kind of (operation) thing for a living.

**

A-HA?

With a few computer key strokes, the (NSA) agency has solved the problem that has bedeviled world powers since at least the time of Caesar Augustus: how to control unruly local leaders, who are the foundation for imperial rule, by ferreting out crucial, often scurrilous, information to make them more malleable. The NSA's global panopticon thus fulfills an ancient dream of empire.

It's about **Blackmail**.

—Surveillance and Scandal, Time-Tested Weapons for U.S. Global Power, Alfred McCoy SOURCE

p.s. We're ALL under surveillance.

I SAW THAT. ~ GOD

1

REENCHANT THE WORLD

"her dream is red and raging.
she will remember
to build something human with it."
—Lucille Clifton, from "Night Vision"

Now is the time, our eyes are open...

There is a river flowing now, very fast. It's great and swift that there are those who will be afraid. They will try and hold onto the shore. They will feel they are being torn apart and suffer greatly. Know that the river has its destination. The elders say we must push off into the middle of the river, keep our eyes open, and our heads above the water. See who is there with you and celebrate. At this point in history, we are to take nothing personally, least of all ourselves, for the moment we do that, our spiritual growth comes to a halt. The time of the lone wolf is over. Gather yourselves. Banish the word "struggle" from your attitude and vocabulary. All that we must do now must be done in a sacred way and in celebration. We are the ones we have been waiting for...

–Hopi Elder Prophecy

Here we go...

What is Late Stage Empire*

Empire still exists in 2021? Yes... and the slippery slopes of the DEEP STATE Military Industrial Complex (MIC), (aka Empire) still use the same old hide and seek game. Hide what they do, hide the money, hide their theft and their looting, of course. The Game? Print more money, make more war, starve whoever you want, and kill more people...

(Top Secret) Militaries run (and loot) the entire world. (Herb-ism)

*An EMPIRE is an aggregate of many separate states or territories under a supreme ruler or oligarchy. This is in contrast to a federation, which is an extensive state voluntarily composed of autonomous states and peoples. 'Empire' and 'colonialism' are used to refer to relationships between a powerful state or society versus a less powerful one.

I think the American Establishment in 2021 is like one of those cheap chocolate Easter bunnies you see in discount store check-out lines. The outer shell is brittle and hard but the center is hollow. The Establishment has built up an extremely formidable wall of defense around itself, but its promises, its rhetoric and the souls of its commanders are hollow and empty. There's nothing new about this— it's how late-stage empires have always worked. **—Author Secret Sun blogger Christopher Loring Knowles**

It wasn't just Black bodies that were scattered across the world—our history was, too.—**Detroit artist Bree Gant**

I t's not enough to reject mainstream politics, we need to reject mainstream culture as well. The propagandists understand that politics is downstream from culture, so we should too. The culture manufacturers in New York and LA are not your friend; **they are an extension of the empire**. We who oppose the empire must reject its manufactured culture with the same disgust with which we reject its political lackeys and news media.

A quick glance around the world will show you that we are very, very, *very* far from this goal, but any time anyone suggests the possibility of taking even one single step in that direction, everyone starts screaming in objection. **—Author Caitlin Johnstone,** *Woke: A Field Guide for Utopia Preppers.*

WHAT IS DEEP STATE?

What is the Deep State? The Deep State is the generals, the war industry, the bankers, the lobbyists, the corporatists, the intelligence agencies, the government bureaucrats and technocrats who actually run both domestic and international policy. The fact is we don't control our own economy. It's controlled by Goldman Sachs and Citibank and JP Morgan Chase. ... And Trump's attraction is that he calls them out often in very vulgar and crude terms. ...they'd rather take the whole system down, which is what they're doing. I think it has misread power. —**Chris Hedges, Dandelion Salad**

Empire NEEDS Religion

Russian Nuclear Orthodoxy: Religion, Politics, and Strategy (Stanford University Press, 2019) by Dmitry Adamsky, a professor at the <u>Interdisciplinary Center Herzliya university</u> in Israel, is a penetrating analysis of the growing influence of the Russian Orthodox Church in Russia's nuclear world—both in the military and the scientific communities.

The state under Vladimir Putin has encouraged the rise of the Russian Orthodox Church but has drawn clear lines of authority to ensure that the church's position in society does exceed what is useful to the Kremlin and does not challenge state policies. Putin has demonstrably identified his regime with the Russian Orthodox Church to such an extent that his policies appear to share certain features with Nicholas I's doctrine of "<u>Orthodoxy, Autocracy, and Nationality</u>."

It would have been helpful if (author) Dmitry Adamsky had provided background to the important historical relationship between the Russian Orthodox Church and the Russian state so that the reader could better understand the context of Adamsky's superb analysis and his extensive narrative of how "… a formerly outcast religion became supported by the state and wormed its way into the most significant wing of one of the most powerful military organizations in the world… within a very short span of time."
—Robert E. Berls Jr.

FYI: Nicholas I emerged as the emperor in the wake of Decembrist revolt; subsequent investigation proved that disloyalty was deeply rooted within the noble estate – the sole foundation of the House of Romanov.[wiki]

READ: https://thebulletin.org/2019/06/blessing-the-holy-icbms-the-russian-orthodox-church-and-putin/

Wait... Who invented Royals?

According to online sources: The concept of royalty is centuries old. It originated with the **feudal systems** of medieval Europe.

CHECK OUT: https://history.howstuffworks.com/historical-figures/royalty1.htm

ROYAL FAMILY MONEY

(2021) In a 'Megxit' interview (with Oprah), in which Prince Harry and Meghan Markle said they were financially cut off from the British monarchy, renews attention on how secretly guarded the royal family's money and assets are. A recent Guardian investigation showed how Queen Elizabeth successfully shielded her private wealth from public view, and Paradise Papers reporting on the monarch and Prince Charles' offshore connections spelled scandal for the clan in 2017. [from International Consortium of Investigative Journalists]

Putin is world's richest man?

Trump wanted to be Putin (and a King) (Herb-ism)

The contemporary (UK) royals have no real power. They serve entirely to enshrine classism in the British nonconstitution. They live in high luxury and low autonomy, cosplaying as their ancestors, and are the subject of constant psychosocial projection from people mourning the loss of empire. They're basically a Rorschach test that the tabloids hold up in order to gauge what level of hysterical *batshittery* their readers are capable of at any moment in time. **—Journalist Patrick Freyne**

LOOK UP: GROOM OF THE STOOL?

Ridgway, Claire. *"What is a Groom of the Stool?"*. the Tudor Society. Tudor Society.

Johnson, Ben. *"Groom of the Stool"*. Historic UK.

HINT: Royal Poop

"Who are the oppressors? The few: the King, the capitalist, and a handful of other overseers and superintendents. Who are the oppressed? The many: the nations of the earth; the valuable personages; the workers; they that make the bread that the soft-handed and idle eat."

—from Philip S. Foner's book *"Mark Twain: Social Critic"*

TWEET-IEST:

Caitlin Johnstone ☐ @caitoz

The monarchy are literally white supremacist pirates. Someone please tell Oprah.

March 8th 2021

115 Retweets **692** Likes

CAITLIN ALSÓ SAID: Poverty is torture. The poverty that capitalist countries bake into their system is the worst kind of all because the victims are made to feel ashamed, and like it's their fault, and like the way out is through simping for their persecutors and working even harder for them.

Royals are just oligarchs who rub your face in it.

Poverty is a big money making industry and many in the "poverty business" don't want to eradicate poverty; they want to control poverty so they can keep getting funding. For many the funding provides a comfortable life for them at the expense of those they claim to be supporting. If poverty becomes obsolete, then the money stops.

—https://BasketsandBeadsKenya.org

In writing *Jesus: A New Vision*, I took a deep dive into what happened to the Roman Empire, and was shocked to find how similar it was to what is happening now.

Beginning around 150 AD, climate change started. It wasn't a rise in carbon dioxide like ours, but a slow decline in solar output. This caused drought in the Mediterranean Basin and across the Steppes of Central Asia, and in many other places. The densely populated Roman Empire began to suffer from chronic malnutrition and one pandemic after another followed because people's immune systems were weakened by starvation.

Having no idea about the way nature works, they gave up on their traditional gods and turned Jesus into Christ and started worshiping him. The pandemics continued, and now the Germans, pressed by the Hungarians who were being pressed by the Huns who were looking for better pasture for their horses, began pushing their way into the empire.

The population now decided that the old gods were not just ineffective but hostile. They went mad with fear, burning the books, smashing the statues, pulling down the temples, in a paroxysm of fanatical destruction that almost destroyed the entire store of knowledge of the ancient world, crushed its religions and transformed the west into a cultural wasteland. Having no idea what was really happening, they blamed their gods for failing them and replaced them with a new one: Christ. The empire collapsed anyway, but Christianity survived and changed the world, as always with great human movements, both for better and for worse.

—Author Whitley Streiber, UNKNOWN COUNTRY.COM

(Image: Jesus Christ, Microsoft Clipart)

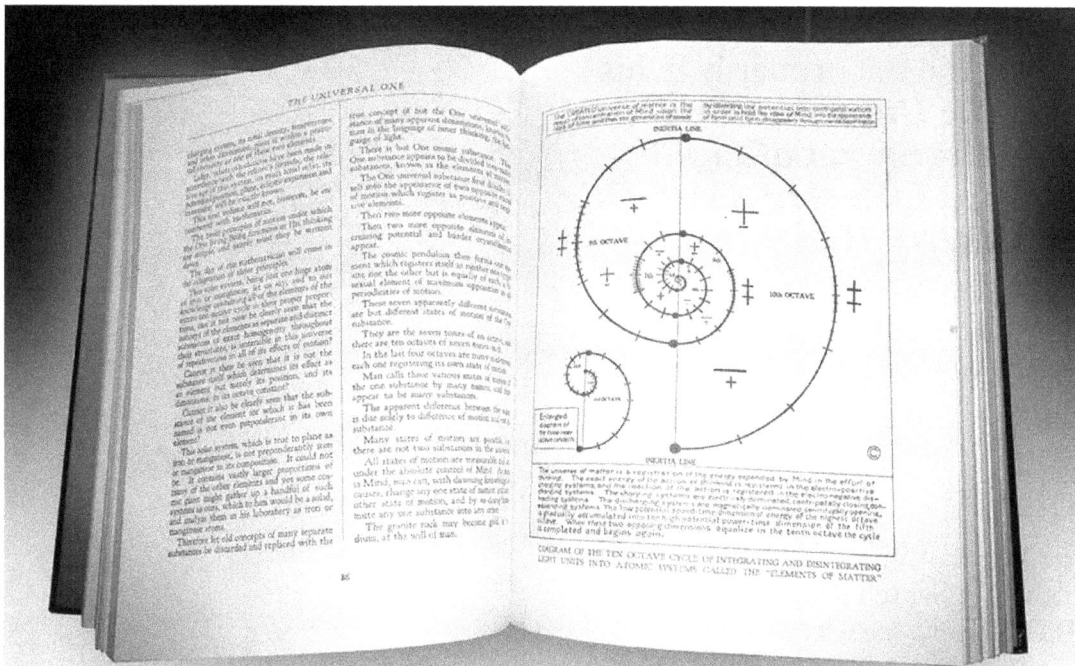

THE UNIVERSAL ONE by Walter Russell

Walter Bowman Russell (May 19, 1871 - May 19, 1963) was an American genius and polymath known for his achievements as a painter, sculptor, author and builder.

In 1963, Walter Cronkite, in the national television evening news, commenting on Russell's death, referred to him as "... the Leonardo da Vinci of our time."

After reading Dr. Russell's book ***The Universal One***, Dr. Nikola Tesla, the great inventor of the world's AC power systems, told him that he should lock his book up for at least a century and perhaps when it is released, after this period of time, the scientific community may be able to understand and accept it.

According to Mr. Russell, the fundamentals of science are so hopelessly wrong and so contrary to nature that nothing but a major surgical operation upon the present primitive beliefs can ever put them in line for a workable cosmogenic synthesis.

His unified physical and spiritual theory is laid out primarily in his books: ***The Universal One*** (1926), ***The Secret of Light*** (1947), and ***THE MESSAGE OF THE DIVINE ILIAD*** (1948 - 1949).

—Dr. Henry and Erika Monteith, www.soulmatecosmology.com

Never heard of Walter Russell? We can guess why... Search his name on YOUTUBE and see why.

Walter Bowman Russell (May 19, 1871 – May 19, 1963) was an impressionist American painter (of the Boston School), sculptor, autodidact and author. His lectures and writing place him firmly in the New Thought Movement (wiki)

THE MAN WHO TAPPED THE SECRETS OF THE UNIVERSE
BY
GLENN CLARK

Vibrational medicine goes back further and stretches across the cultures of early humanity; it is not just the arena of the Middle East and the Mediterranean. 40,000 years ago in Australia, the world's oldest wind instrument, the 'yidaki'—now known as the 'didgeridoo'—was used to heal broken bones, muscle tears, and illnesses.

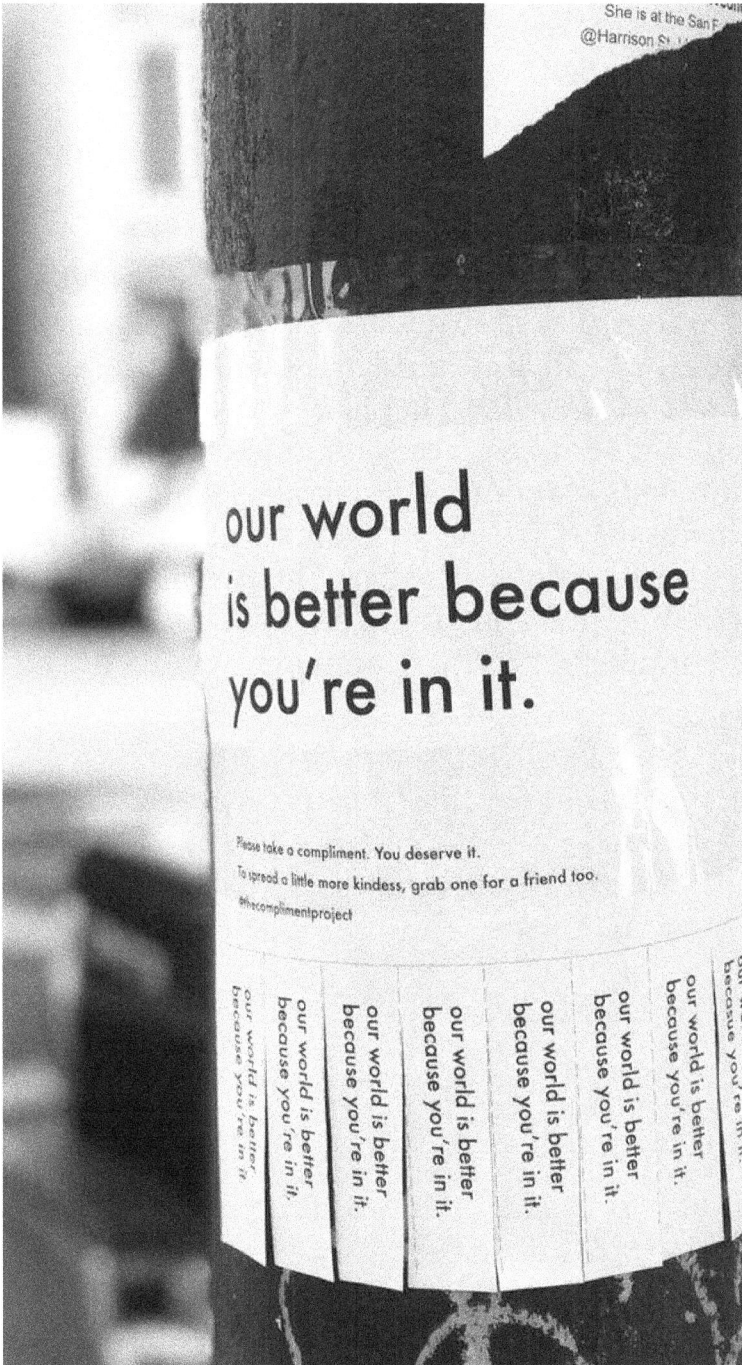

"People have a hard time accepting anything that overwhelms them." —Musician Bob Dylan on sacrifice, the unconscious mind, and the ideal environment for creative work…

Human trafficking and modern-day slavery are umbrella terms —often used interchangeably—that refers to the exploitation of individuals through threat or use of force, coercion, abduction, fraud, and/or deception. 40 million people annually are impacted by one of these types of trafficking globally. It includes the practices of forced labor, debt bondage, domestic servitude, forced marriage, sex trafficking, child sex trafficking, and the recruitment and use of child soldiers, among others. The most common forms of exploitation are forced labor, which, according to the International Labor Organization, impacts 24.9 million people a year—16 million in private sector exploitation, 4 million in state-sanctioned forced labor, and 4.8 million in sex trafficking—and forced marriage, which enslaves 15.4 million individuals. The ILO estimates that forced labor generates $150 billion in illegal profits each year. The two most commonly known forms of human trafficking are sexual exploitation and forced labor. (From HumanTraffickingSearch.org) (2021)

(My photo: African wood art sculpture)

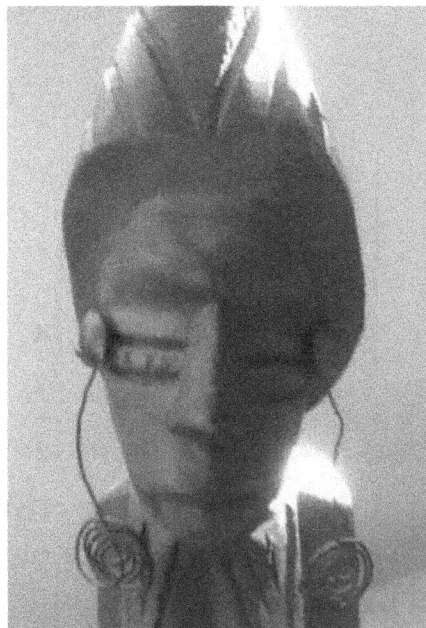

I've been hiding. At first it was politics. The 2016 election and subsequent scandal upon horror upon disaster have left me feeling scraped raw and staked out on the mountaintop for buzzards to eat my intestines. So, yeah. I started hiding from Facebook and Twitter, because most days it felt like the news was just pouring acid into open wounds. I've read blog posts by other authors who said that they've had trouble writing in this political climate—they've had trouble feeling like anything they do could possibly make a difference.

—Author April White, 2018

(My 2021 Photo: Sunbow on I-91)

"All the plastic that's ever been created still exists because it can't be destroyed, it doesn't decompose... I thought that was an interesting premise for a puppet show: someone discovering our trash in the future, and misinterpreting its significance in our lives, and its actual function."—Upcycle Artist Robin Frohardt ((https://www.robinfrohardt.com))

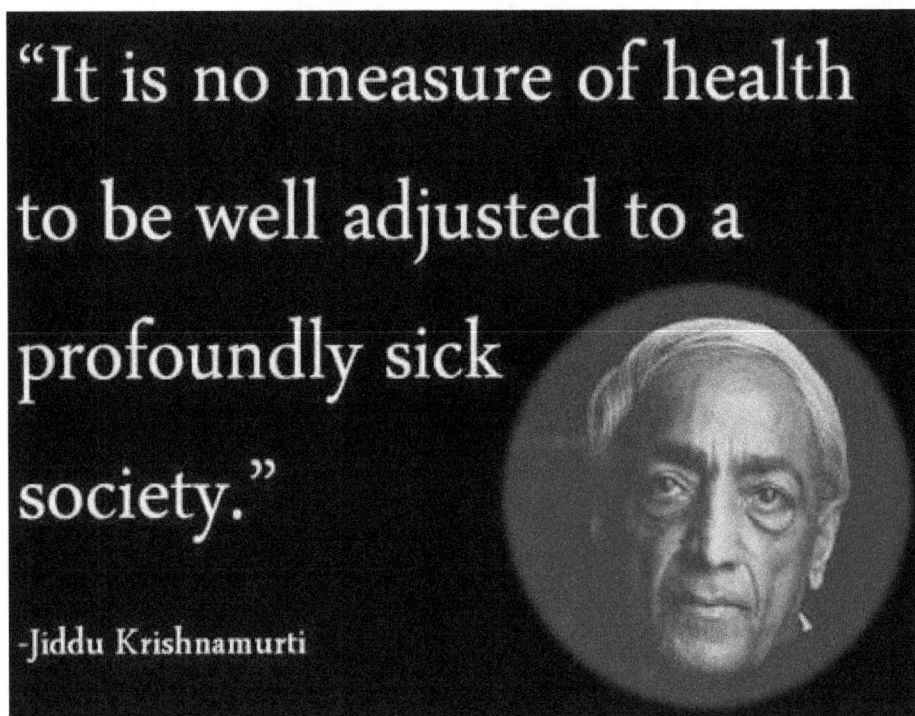

"It is no measure of health to be well adjusted to a profoundly sick society."

-Jiddu Krishnamurti

(Clipart)

An estimated $57 billion in gold, silver, platinum, and other precious metals hidden in old devices (electronics) was sent to landfills in 2019 alone. (online statistic)

(My 2020 Photo: Orbits)

Close your eyes, let your hands and nerve-ends drop, stop breathing for 3 seconds, listen to the silence inside the illusion of the world, and you will remember the lesson you forgot, which was taught in immense milky way soft cloud innumerable worlds long ago and not even at all. It is all one vast awakened thing. I call it the golden eternity. It is perfect.

—Kerouac sent one such letter to his first wife, Edie Kerouac Parker, in late January of 1957, a decade after their marriage had been annulled. Found in *The Portable Jack Kerouac* (*public library*)—an altogether terrific treasure trove of his stories, poems, letters, and essays on Buddhism—the missive is nothing short of exquisite.

Hallucination?

Alan Watts puts it this way:

I wonder what you mean when you use the word I.

I've been very interested in this problem for a long, long time. And I've come to the conclusion that what most civilized people mean by that word is a hallucination—that is to say a false sense of personal identity that is at complete variance with the facts of nature.

And as a result of having a false sense of identity, we act in a way that is inappropriate to our natural environment. And when that inappropriate way of action is magnified by a very powerful technology, we swiftly begin to see the results of a profound discord between man and nature.

As is well known, we are now in the process of destroying our environment as a result of an attempt to conquer it and master it. And we have not realized therefore that our environment is not something other than ourselves.

In assuming that it is, we have made a great mistake and are now paying the price for it.

(**Alan Wilson Watts** (6 January 1915 – 16 November 1973) was a British philosopher, writer and speaker known for interpreting and popularising Buddhism, Taoism, and Hinduism for a Western audience)

BLURSDAY?
Emerging?

—April 2020—How many days have I been in lockdown?

Since Friday the 13, March 2020. Oh hell I remember the exact day.

What day is it now? I don't know. It's Blursday again... It feels like an eternity since March 2020.

Back then we went out three days in a row on errands and I cannot begin to tell you how wonderful to see springtime blooming trees and little yellow birds and my friends at the local post office. We call all our errands our mini-dates.

I sure miss seeing people, and hugging people.

I'm gonna quote Virginia Woolf: "I am made and remade continually. Different people draw different words from me."

When I heard Native Poet Laureate Joy Harjo speak online, she said it perfectly: **"We are emerging—in an emergency."**

Just for fun, I looked at what a Debt Jubilee would mean—a forgiveness of all debt, rarely mentioned anywhere.

The federal government is free to print all the money it needs to pay government debts.

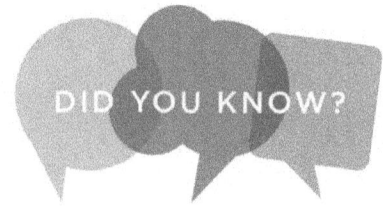

(Wait, WHAT???) TRUE!

Private households are different. The only ways out of **private debt** are to pay it, to default, or to have it forgiven with a **Debt Jubilee**. A growing movement says debt forgiveness for developing nations would "free up resources to tackle urgent health, social and economic crises."

DEBT JUBILEE? Whoa! Hurry it up, please… (and universal basic income: <u>UBI</u>)

And lastly: The mightiest military in the world didn't see a plague coming? Really? What do we pay you for? You made billions of bullets and bombs but didn't make enough protective gear for doctors or the public or have adequate testing and face masks? Really?

Our past president was dumb and worried about reelection, so he didn't want more plague virus testing. That was it. It would make him look bad.

TRUMP already looked bad.

(Homeless: Microsoft Clipart)

AMERI CA IS NOT FULL

Clear Coherent People are a Danger to the Chaos People. Be Safe!

EVERYTHING PLASTIC CAN BE MADE FROM HEMP.

AND PLASTIC MADE FROM HEMP IS BIO-DEGRADABLE.

THE MIND UNLEASHED

IMAGE: https://themindunleashed.com/

Who else knows about this HEIST?

FUNNY MONEY & MALWARE—Biggest Heist of the Century (2015)?

Hackers may have perpetrated the biggest bank robbery of all time when they gained access to the computer systems of 100 banks in 30 countries. They may have gotten away with close to a billion dollars, report David Sanger and Nicole Perlroth for the *NYT,* but nobody can say for sure because "no bank has come forward acknowledging the theft." (via Bill Moyers)_ (in 2015) Who knew?

BIGGEST BANK HEIST in 2021? (oh no...not again!)

(International Consortium of Investigative Journalists) —Ihor Kolomoisky, a powerful Ukrainian billionaire under investigation for allegedly orchestrating one of the biggest bank heists in history, is barred from entering the U.S. The oligarch and several associates are accused of funneling hundreds of millions in fraudulent loans obtained from Ukraine's largest bank, which he co-owned, through shell companies into the U.S.—where the money was plowed into real estate.
Our reporting showed how Kolomoisky secretly amassed a Midwest property empire with the help of Deutsche Bank—and the toll this took on local communities, factory conditions, and steelworkers. The investigation shed light on the human impact that dirty money can have when landlords take control of buildings and workplaces to clean their cash.
U.S. prosecutors are now seeking to seize some of the properties that Kolomoisky and others purchased in their real estate buying spree.

...Oligarchism is parasitism... all the rest may be noise.—*Full Spectrum Domino*

God Bless the United States Postal Service

Regardless of rain, snow—or even a worldwide pandemic—our mail carrier makes a 100 stops like this every day. We recently learned that he was injured on the job, so we make this post in honor of him. We really appreciate and value his kind and patient demeanor, especially during our busiest shipping days. Eighth Generation needs USPS. Our brick and mortar store at Pike Place Market in Seattle has been closed for 6 months, forcing us to depend solely on online sales. This means that we rely on shipping in order to complete every single sale. At a time when our small business is more dependent on USPS than ever before, we are scared by the recent attacks on this essential part of our distribution chain.

(and image) —https://eighthgeneration.com/blogs/blog/we-support-the-united-states-postal-service

Stone "rakan" statues in Kyoto, the ancient capital of colored leaves in Japan (@you_ji_low via @atlasobscura/Instagram)

The era of greed and violence—is a reality throughout much of the world today. Corruption, greed, poverty, consumerism, power to the few, and injustice are predominant characteristics of our civilization accompanied by a great technological advancement that has become a weapon for mass destruction and a tool for suppressing resistance. Whether beings from the past will interfere or not, one thing is for sure, life cannot continue in this way forever.—**John Black**

HOW BAD? VERY VERY BAD

"The plans to beam highly penetrative 5G milliwave radiation at us from space must surely be one of the greatest follies ever conceived of by mankind. There will be nowhere safe to live."—Olga Sheean, former WHO employee and author of 'No Safe Place'

Read EMERGENCY IN THE HEAVENS:

https://www.cellphonetaskforce.org/wp-content/uploads/2020/10/Emergency-in-the-Heavens.pdf

On April 11, 1862, Henry Brooks Adams, grandson of the sixth American president, wrote, "I firmly believe that before many centuries more, science will be the master of man. The engines he will have invented will be beyond his strength to control. Someday science may have the existence of mankind in its power, and the human race commit suicide by blowing up the world."

(Image: Road Sign, Amish in Pennsylvania)

talk
to god

listen.

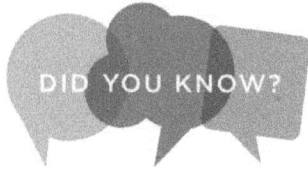

DID YOU KNOW **THIS?**

How long can a chicken live without its head?
About two years.

What do chameleons do?
They don't change color to match the background. Never have; never will. Complete myth. Utter fabrication. Total Lie. They change color as a result of different emotional states.

How many legs does a centipede have?
Not a hundred.

How many toes has a two-toed sloth?
It's either six or eight.

Who was the first American president?
Peyton Randolph.

What were George Washington's false teeth made from?
Mostly hippopotamus.

What was James Bond's favorite drink?
Not the vodka martini.

—from The Book of General Ignorance

Then I found this: The last few hours of sleep are the most important. Football was so brutal in 1905, 18 players lost their lives.

What are some of your amazing discoveries?

You just wait until I build my TIME MACHINE. All I need is $2 trillion. I already have some Nigerian bitcoin investors, including a prince! —JB on Secret Sun blog

GHOST DNA?

This is FASCINATING! Everyone I know is talking about DNA tests and ancestry. According to a new report: About 50,000 years ago, ancient humans in what is now West Africa apparently procreated with another group of ancient humans that scientists didn't know existed. There aren't any bones or ancient DNA to prove it, but researchers say the evidence is in the genes of modern West Africans. They analyzed genetic material from hundreds of people from Nigeria and Sierra Leone and found signals of what they call "ghost" DNA from an unknown ancestor.

The findings on ghost DNA, published in the journal Science Advances, further complicate the picture of how *Homo sapiens*—or modern humans—evolved away from other human relatives.

The scientists analyzed the genomes of 405 West Africans. Sriram Sankararaman, a computational biologist at UCLA, says they used a statistical model to flag parts of the DNA. The technique "goes along a person's genome and pulls out chunks of DNA which we think are likely to have come from a population that is not modern human."

NPR had this story:

50,000 Years Ago—Who Slept With Whom?

The unusual DNA found in West Africa isn't associated with either Neanderthals or Denisovans. Sankararaman and his study co-author, Arun Durvasula, think it comes from a yet-to-be-discovered group.

"We don't have a clear identity for this archaic group," Sankararaman says. "That's why we use the term 'ghost.' It doesn't seem to be particularly closely related to the groups from which we have genome sequences from."

The scientists think the interbreeding happened about 50,000 years ago, roughly the same time that Neanderthals were breeding with modern humans elsewhere in the world. It's not clear whether there was a single interbreeding "event," though, or whether it happened over an extended period of time.

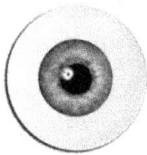

The unknown group "appears to have split off from the ancestors of modern humans a little before when Neanderthals split off from our ancestors," he says.

So what happened to this mysterious group of ancient humans? Scientists aren't totally sure. They might have died off, or they might have eventually been completely subsumed into modern humans.

READ: (https://www.npr.org/sections/health-shots/2013/12/18/252046939/mixing-it-up-50-000-years-ago-who-slept-with-whom)

Image: Walking Feet, Death to Stock Photos, royalty free images

"Most species do their own evolving, making it up as they go along, which is the way Nature intended. And this is all very natural and organic and in tune with mysterious cycles of the cosmos, which believes that there's nothing like millions of years of really frustrating trial and error to give a species moral fiber and, in some cases, backbone." **—Terry Pratchett, Reaper Man**

(My Photo: Bedroom Light)

"No man has ever yet been able to purchase happiness, prosperity, peace or love with any other coin than happiness, peace and love. The price of love is love. The price of greed is agony."—Walter Russell, 1930

After decades of work on reforming corporations to be more sustainable, we both came to understand that we can't change the way business does business unless we change the way **money makes money**. Given our perilous situation with the unfolding environmental breakdown, this change is more urgent than ever. So what might we do? We can move our money to building societies. But that won't reform the big banks.—*Professor Jem Bendell and Rabbi Jeffrey Newman*- Regenerative Culture

"It's not always just the heart. Sometimes your mind breaks as well."

– r.h. Sin

**

White collar crime? Blood Money?

Mafia manages the military?

White-collar crime *is* violent crime: It's called blood money for a reason. Over the last 40 years, white-collar crime, state crime, and organized crime have merged to the point that criminal networks now control governments, which allow them to redefine what they are doing as legal, exonerate themselves, and persecute those who seek to uphold the law. The mafia manages the military, the crooks control the courts. —**brilliant author Sara Kenzior**

I'm mad as hell and I'm not going to take it anymore. —**Networks' HOWARD BEALE**

**

STAR SPANGLED BANNER?

No one sings this verse? I never even knew about it! The third verse of the National Anthem goes like this:

And where is that band who so vauntingly swore,
  That the havoc of war and the battle's confusion
  A home and a Country should leave us no more?
  Their blood has wash'd out their foul footstep's
  pollution.
  No refuge could save the hireling and slave
From the terror of flight or the gloom of the grave,
And the star-spangled banner in triumph doth wave
O'er the land of the free and the home of the brave.

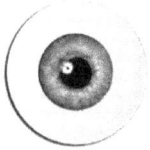

"When you're writing, you're trying to find out something which you don't know. The whole language of writing for me is finding out what you don't want to know, what you don't want to find out. But something forces you to anyway." **—Author James Baldwin**

**

Seaspiracy is the groundbreaking **Netflix** Original documentary which seeks to expose the fishing industries impact on the world's oceans and challenge notions of sustainable fishing. WATCH IT! Visit: https://www.seaspiracy.org

OUR BRAINS (and Jaws) ARE REALLY SHRINKING (really)

The "evolution of humankind" timelines in natural history museums typically span hundreds of thousands of years and end with the earliest evidence of written language, a few thousand years B.C. But the truth is that our bodies are still evolving—our brains are shrinking, our elbows are narrowing. And our faces are still changing too, leading to dramatic changes in our teeth, noses, and jaws. The implications of shrinking modern skulls are more than aesthetic. Our smaller faces do the most harm in one area crucial to physical and mental health: our ability to get a good night's sleep.**—Katherine Reynolds Lewis, One Zero Medium**

"Every five seconds a child under ten dies from hunger, 57,000 people every day, a billion are severely malnourished, and this is happening on a planet that is overflowing with wealth and that could actually feed twelve billion people."—*We Let the Third World Starve—The Disaster Can Be Stopped*, author Jean Ziegler

The most goggled word in 2020: Pandemic

The Best Word of 2020: Mutual Aid Society

Mutual aid is arguably as ancient as human culture. People in every society in every time period have worked together to ensure their communities can survive...

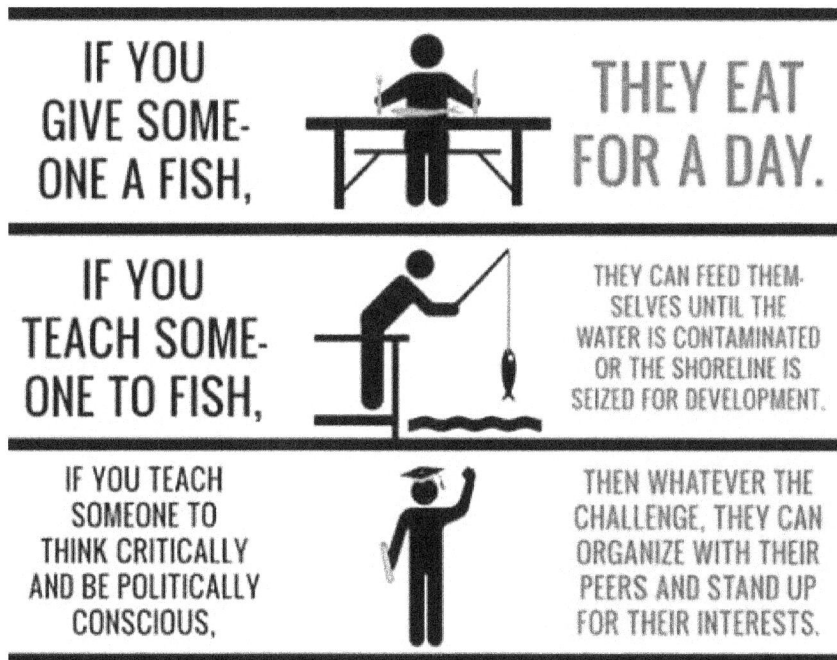

IF YOU GIVE SOME-ONE A FISH, THEY EAT FOR A DAY.

IF YOU TEACH SOME-ONE TO FISH, THEY CAN FEED THEM-SELVES UNTIL THE WATER IS CONTAMINATED OR THE SHORELINE IS SEIZED FOR DEVELOPMENT.

IF YOU TEACH SOMEONE TO THINK CRITICALLY AND BE POLITICALLY CONSCIOUS, THEN WHATEVER THE CHALLENGE, THEY CAN ORGANIZE WITH THEIR PEERS AND STAND UP FOR THEIR INTERESTS.

"It's peculiar and unnerving in a way to see so many young people walking around with cellphones and iPods in their ears and so wrapped up in media and video games. It robs them of their self-identity. It's a shame to see them so tuned out to real life. Of course they are free to do that, as if that's got anything to do with freedom. The cost of liberty is high, and young people should understand that before they start spending their life with all those gadgets." **—Nobel Prize Winner Musician Bob Dylan**

# #

...think about your childhood bed and how much weird energy had been in that place. All your imagination. It reminds me of a Bob Dylan story. Apparently, when he's touring he likes to go to the homes of other songwriters. In Canada he found the place where Neil Young grew up. Imagine you live in Neil Young's childhood home and Bob Dylan stands on your front porch to see the bedroom. The owner said that Dylan just stood there and went, "That's where Neil Young dreamed all his dreams." I guess that's what you're doing as a writer—you're trying to be the ghost of yourself. **—Writer Scott McClanahan**

BUMMER

I really love this guy! Technologist and philosopher oracle Jaron Lanier, a virtual reality pioneer and early internet evangelist who isn't on Reddit, Facebook, Twitter, or Instagram, contends that you should just quit social media.

Go cold turkey.

In his book, *Ten Arguments for Deleting Your Social Media Accounts Right Now*, Lanier argues that engaging on the internet makes us feel bad because systems are designed to manipulate us by measuring our interests, anticipating our desires, modifying our behavior, and creating opportunities for advertisers.

He's developed a simple acronym to sum up the sinister purpose of tech companies that brought us the platforms we're hooked on and their effect on us—**BUMMER. It stands for Behaviors of Users Modified and Made into Empires for Rent.**

Read Lanier's books—2010's *You Are Not a Gadget,* 2013's *Who Owns the Future?,* 2017's *Dawn of the New Everything,* and 2018's *Ten Arguments*

✳

"Hate only hatred. The extreme limit of wisdom—that's what the public calls madness." —Poet, playwright, novelist, designer, filmmaker, visual artist and critic Jean Cocteau

Join the <u>UN's Pledge to Pause campaign</u>, which uses behavioral science to combat the spread of misinformation. The simple act of pausing interrupts our emotional response so we can ask: "WHO made it, WHAT is the source, WHEN was it published and WHY are you sharing. (PauseButton: Micosoft Clipart)

*

Life is a shitstorm, in which art is our only umbrella. Literature creates a fraternity within human diversity and eclipses the frontiers erected among men and women by ignorance, ideologies, religions, languages, and stupidity. — **Peruvian novelist Mario Vargas Llosa, one of the writing giants of our time, Nobel Prize in Literature in 2010** (Einstein clip art : Pinterest)

"Art is standing with one hand extended into the universe and one hand extended into the world, and letting ourselves be a conduit for passing energy." --Albert Einstein

(My 2020 Photo: Orb illusion)

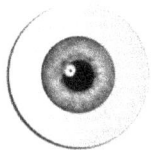

*

"The books of mine I like best are the ones I hardly recognize as products of my labor after they appear. That is, they come from some uncharted place inside that is smarter and more daring and more interesting than I am."—**the late American author, academic and film critic Jonathan Baumbach**

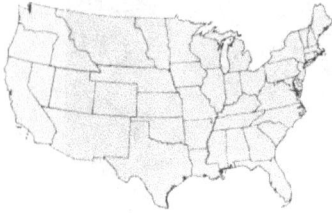

America in 1857 was a simmering stew of con artists, flim-flammers and grifters exploiting the naive, the trusting and the credulous, and that remains the case in 2019. **We now inhabit a world where virtually everything is a con.** And today virtually everything is fake, a con designed to trick or distract the marks (us) from the looting, plundering and predation of those running the con for their own self-interest. **—Charles Hugh Smith (_Pathfinding our Destiny: Preventing the Final Fall of Our Democratic Republic_)**

My message is essentially: "Embrace the mystery. It will feed your mind."**—Secret Sun blogger and author Christopher Knowles**   (My Photo: 2020 Moon Glow)

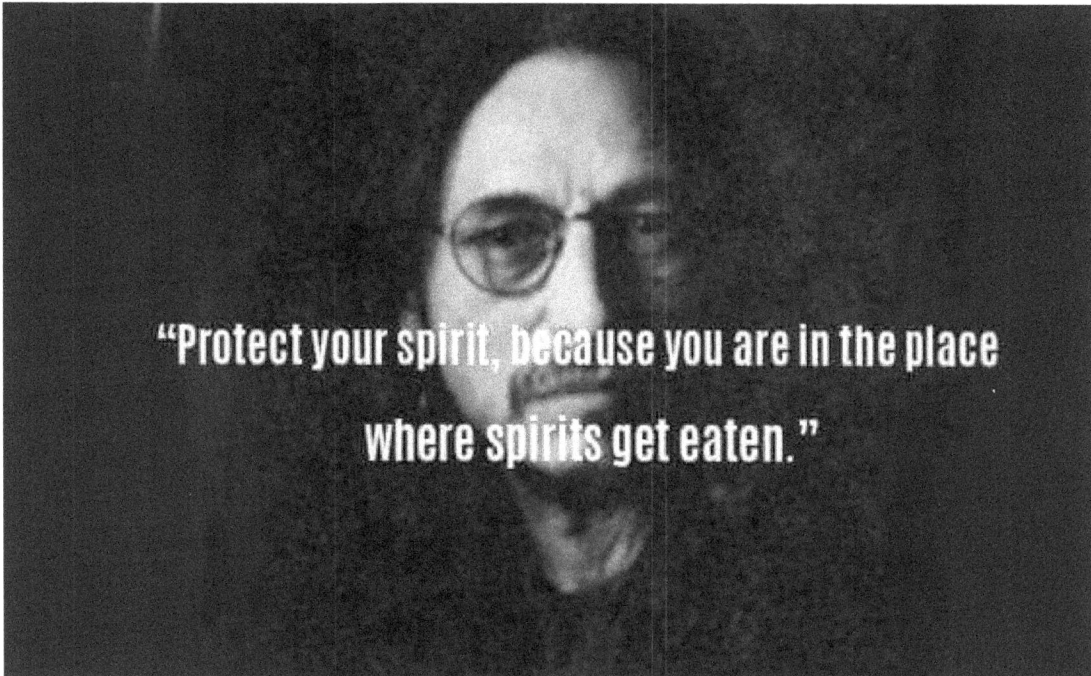

"Protect your spirit, because you are in the place where spirits get eaten."

(See more from John Trudell in Section 4)

"I'd like to share a revelation during my time here. It came to me when I tried to classify your species. I realized that you're not actually mammals. Every mammal on this planet instinctively develops a natural equilibrium with the surrounding environment but you humans do not. You move to an area and you multiply and multiply until every natural resource is consumed. The only way you can survive is to spread to another area. There is another organism on this planet that follows the same pattern. Do you know what it is? A virus. Human beings are a disease, a cancer of this planet. You are a plague, and we are the cure." **—Agent Smith (MATRIX MOVIE)**

THE DEMON-HAUNTED WORLD

immediately. *Not* explaining science seems to me perverse. When you're in love, you want to tell the world. This book is a personal statement, reflecting my lifelong love affair with science.

But there's another reason: science is more than a body of knowledge; it is a way of thinking. I have a foreboding of an America in my children's or grandchildren's time - when the United States is a service and information economy; when nearly all the key manufacturing industries have slipped away to other countries; when awesome technological powers are in the hands of a very few, and no one representing the public interest can even grasp the issues; when the people have lost the ability to set their own agendas or knowledgeably question those in authority; when, clutching our crystals and nervously consulting our horoscopes, our critical faculties in decline, unable to distinguish between what feels good and what's true, we slide, almost without noticing, back into superstition and darkness. The dumbing down of America is most evident in the slow decay of substantive content in the enormously influential media, the 30-second sound bites (now down to 10 seconds or less), lowest common denominator programming, credulous presentations on pseudoscience and superstition, but especially a kind of celebration of ignorance. As ~~~~~~~~ ~~~~~ ~~~ video cassette rental in America is the

(scanned book)

Unidentified Flying Object on Navajoland

(my screenshot) UFO Spotted on NBC News Segment (August 2020)

2020 Poet Laureate Joy Harjo:

Poetry is one way to access memory, to hold memory. In this digital and cellular age, we don't have to remember anything, not even our telephone numbers. You push a button, you click on a keyboard, touch a screen, it appears that all sorts of memory is available. You have access to libraries and to different collections, and you don't have to remember anything. What do we give up? Is there a middle road? You won't be able to hear your soul, or find the impetus to grow it. The stories, the people—what happens to memory and your relationship to memory, or rather the path of your own existence on a planet that is essentially you? What happens when our stories and our presence becomes reduced to sound bites and selfies?

Never help a person who doesn't help anybody else...

Take a breath of the new dawn and make it a part of you...

The dead add their strength and counsel to the living...

—Hopi Proverbs

"I will follow the white man's trail. I will make him my friend, but I will not bend my back to his burdens. I will be cunning as a coyote.

I will ask him to help me understand his ways, then I will prepare the way for my children, and their children. The Great Spirit has shown me—a day will come when they will outrun the white man in his own shoes." — Tasunke Ota, Oglala Lakota

"There are gonna be two roads. A muddy road, and an easy road. The rich kid takes the easy road and the poor kid takes the muddy road. The kid on the muddy road builds up strength to become a warrior." —Robert Looks Twice, Oglala Lakota

(IMAGE: coyote: Microsoft Clipart)

"The only biological difference in the human race is between male and female and no matter the alleged identity group diversity, humans have had and continue to have no problem at all at mating, pro-creating, or just having recreational sex with one another across all alleged and artificial divides of nations, religions or ethnicity. Tall, short, rotund and thin humans are not separate races except to the **tragically mis-informed or propaganda barraged believers** and the same is true for skin tones and language /cultural differences. " —Truthaholics Blog June 2, 2019

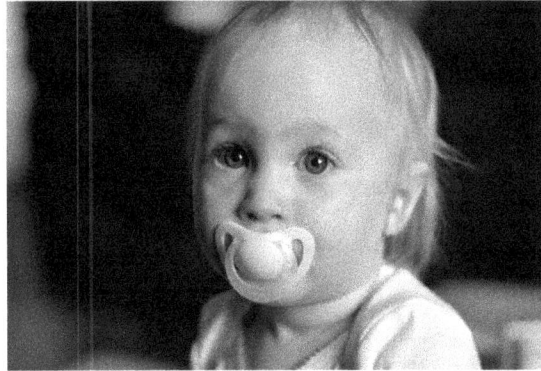

https://truthaholics.wordpress.com/

Truth has been replaced by a new currency: **dirt**. In 1967, in an essay called "Truth and Politics," which was published in *The New Yorker*, Hannah Arendt warned where mendacity can lead. "The result of a consistent and total substitution of lies for factual truth is not that the lies will now be accepted as truth, and the truth be defamed as lies, but that the sense by which we take our bearings in the real world—and the category of truth vs. falsehood is among the mental means to this end—is being destroyed."

What did the bunny rabbit say to the other bunny rabbit?

(Write your brilliant answer here)

My Guess:

Bunny 1: What do rabbits have that nothing else in the world has?
Bunny 2: Baby rabbits.

(Bunny: Microsoft Clip Art)

QUESTIONS:

Ask yourself here

(My Photo 2021) Reaching to the Heavens

"PLANTS" Word Search—how many can you find? (circle letters)

```
N Y U H F O X G L O V E B F
R A O Y P P O P S E R I S M
C R E S S C T U T E N A A J
J R M S L D T O G E V N N P
B O D O U O O N N N D I E C
N W V P L R I A P R E S H F
A E R Y M G B A A L N E R C
R V T U A A R K L U R W G L
X V L T E S E U D V A F N I
T A R L L E M S I A N N E S
R H F E L E C L V I H R S A
G Y Y M T A G Y L N P L N B
Y R A M T S O C A I N N I Z
P B G G E Z A E Y B D E G A
```

///2///

COSMIC GLUE

"I begin, a sentence lover. I'm forever delighted, then delighted all over, at the things sentences can trip and trick you into saying, into seeing. I'm astonished—just plain tickled!—at the sharp turns and tiny tremors they can whip your thoughts across. I'm entranced by their lollop and flow, their prickles and points. Poetry is made of words, Mallarmé told us a hundred years back. But I write prose. And prose is made of sentences."—**Author Samuel R. Delany (African American science fiction author and genius)**

FIRST LESSONS:

LET ME TEACH YOU SOME THINGS

Lesson Number One:

When spoken out loud, words transform into frequencies and create vibrations that can direct Energy.

Words are not just elements of speech or writing...words have power. Words are power.

Words are the art of directing and controlling energy.

Once you know that, this is how words (along with sound) is used to direct energy,

She wasn't looking
for a knight,
she was looking
for a sword.

- atticus

you will know that words can be as powerful, or even more powerful than swords.

When you move the letter "s" in "words" to the front, you get "sword."

This is not an accident.

Your awareness is one of the most powerful spiritual powers **you** have.

Manna: Scholars, soldiers, and scientists have long puzzled over the supernatural substance called manna. It spontaneously regenerated each morning, even in convenient double quantities on the day before the Sabbath.
https://www.atlasobscura.com/articles/is-manna-real

Lesson Number Two: (from the Matrix Movie)

Morpheus: The Matrix is everywhere. It is all around us, even now in this very room. You can see it when you look out your window or when you turn on your television. You can feel it when you go to work, when you go to church, when you pay your taxes. It is the world that has been pulled over your eyes to blind you from the truth.

Neo: What truth?

Morpheus: That you are a slave, Neo. Like everyone else, you were born into bondage, born into a prison that you cannot smell, or taste, or touch. A prison for your mind.

[The *Matrix* series includes a trilogy of feature films, all of which were written and directed by the Wachowskis and produced by Joel Silver]

" New knowledge is the most valuable commodity on earth. The more truth we have to work with, the richer we become. "

Kurt Vonnegut

(Cat's Cradle)

DID YOU KNOW?
The Egyptians used certain resonant vowel sounds in their ancient rituals; these vowels were considered so sacred that they were banned from everyday language and did not appear in the written language of hieroglyphics. Further, Egyptians used an instrument called a 'sistrum' during ceremonies, a rattle with metal disks attached to it, which has been shown to create exceptionally high levels of ultrasound. Native American powwows, with drumming, chanting, and singing, have been used to treat mental and physical illness for many thousands of years.

Lesson Number Three:

Ho'oponopono Teaching (Hawaii)

I love you,

I'm sorry,

please forgive me,

and thank you.

WIKI:

After Morrnah Simeona's death in 1992, her former student and administrator, Ihaleakala Hew Len, co-authored a book with Joe Vitale called *Zero Limits* referring to Simeona's Ho'oponopono teachings. Len makes no claim to be a *kahuna*. In contrast to Simeona's teachings, the book brings the new idea that the main objective of Ho'oponopono is getting to the "zero state — it's where we have zero limits. No memories. No identity. "To reach this state, which Len called 'Self-I-Dentity thru Ho'oponopono', includes using the mantra, "I love you. I'm sorry. Please forgive me. Thank you."

It is based on Len's idea of 100% responsibility, taking responsibility for everyone's actions, not only for one's own. If one would take complete responsibility for one's life, then everything one sees, hears, tastes, touches, or in any way experiences would be one's responsibility because it is in one's life. The problem would not be with our external reality, it would be with ourselves. Total Responsibility, according to Hew Len, advocates that everything exists as a projection from inside the human being. (wiki)

Soulmates: You have more than one in life, for there are different ones for different things. There are musical taste soulmates, best friend soulmates, let's get coffee soulmates, artist soulmates, etc. etc. The romantic soulmate is one aspect of this notion. Never forget that. –on Pinterest

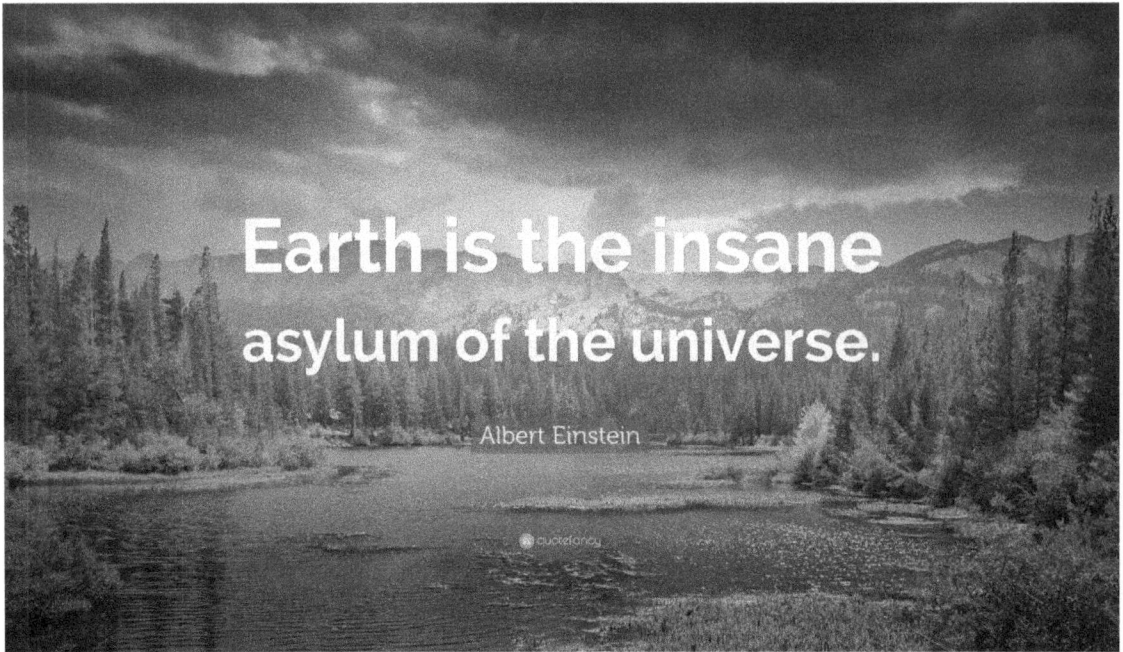

Earth is the insane asylum of the universe.

Albert Einstein

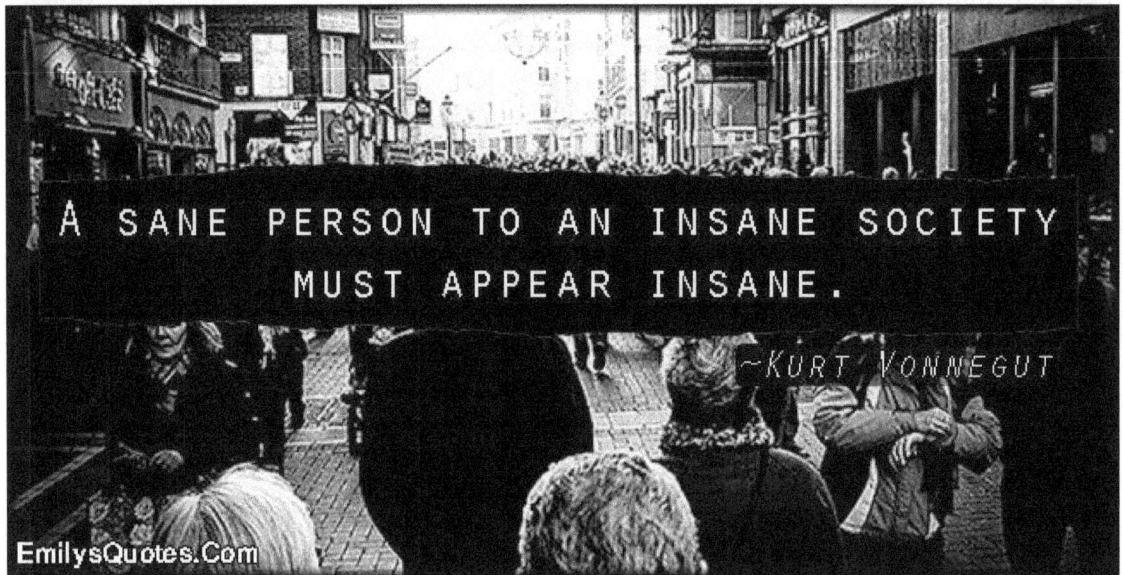

A SANE PERSON TO AN INSANE SOCIETY
MUST APPEAR INSANE.

~KURT VONNEGUT

EmilysQuotes.Com

Who changed the frequency?

Even More Lessons:

THE FIRST MYSTICAL LAW

THERE IS ONLY NOW

The heart of so many mystical disciplines is "Stay fully present." Learn to keep your spirit fully in focus, so that you know where "all of you" is at all times.

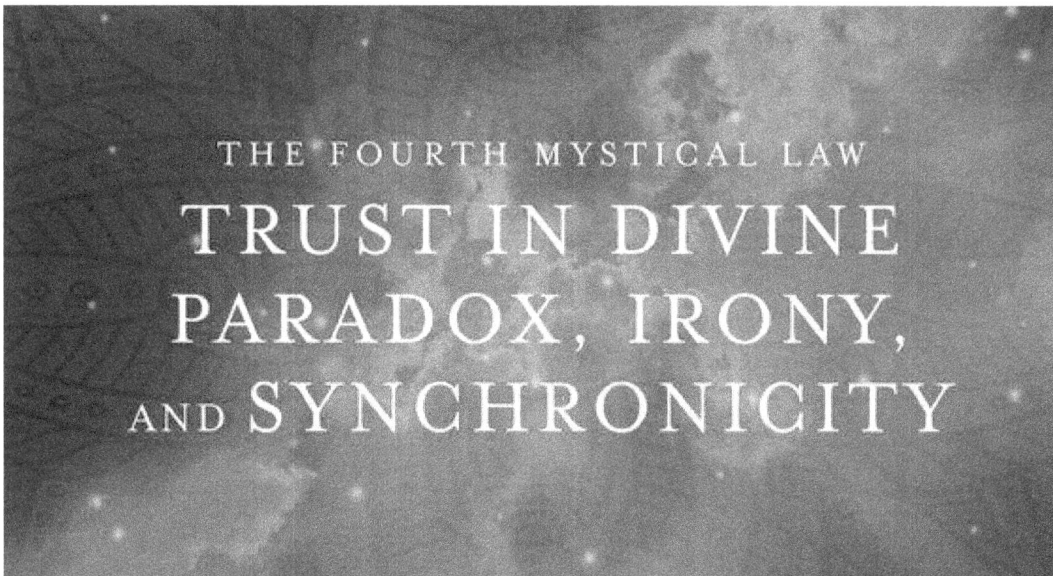

THE FOURTH MYSTICAL LAW

TRUST IN DIVINE PARADOX, IRONY, AND SYNCHRONICITY

Ironic events along with paradoxical ones stand out in our lives, calling us to notice them. Change arrives because you need to move forward, not retreat to the past.

Read them all: https://www.myss.com/category/mystical-laws/

Water is Life #NoDAPL

No Dakota Access Pipeline Protest Art (GRAPHIC: Christy Belcourt)

The Legacy of Cosmic Glue (number 2):

Acts of Cruelty

If you intentionally

Hurt

Harm

Injure

Manipulate

Kill

Your descendants will be punished for your actions.

An elder explained to me if you violate someone's will, when you treat others with cruelty, violence, physical assault, seduction, sexual assault, or murder, the person or persons who do that to another person will not personally suffer. No. Their child/children/grandchildren will pay the price, including sickness, assault, suffering and even death.

As we know, not all criminals and crimes are prosecuted. If you treat people with kindness, and be of pure heart, you can prevent and stop further karmic retribution from the acts of cruelty from your current and distant ancestors, even from past centuries.

DO NOT IGNORE the past and the genocides and cruelties.

You are paying for them with YOUR life. Future Generations will pay for YOUR crimes. This is not widely understood.

An apology will never do.

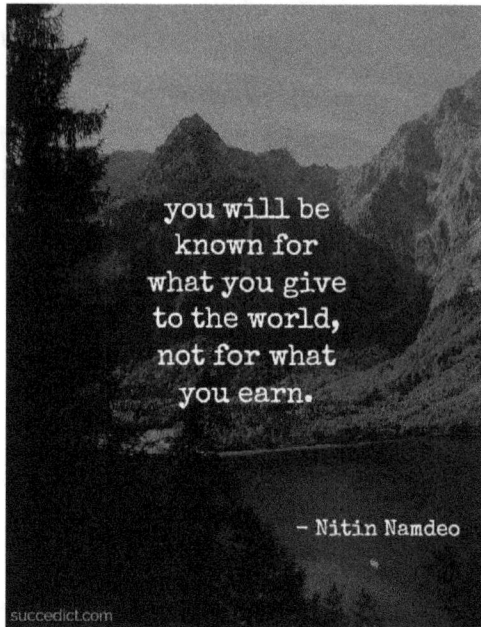

you will be
known for
what you give
to the world,
not for what
you earn.

— Nitin Namdeo

succedict.com

The Legacy of Cosmic Glue (number 3)

Generosity

Be Extremely Generous
(Did I say extremely?)
(I did! I do mean that…)

I <u>akisaed</u> (shouted in happiness). I had not been forgotten— the Lakota values of generosity and faith resonated from home. <u>Lakolwicohan</u> (the real way of life) has survived. —<u>Lydia Whirlwind Soldier</u> (*Wancantognaka:* The continuing Lakota tradition of generosity—<u>Volume 7, No. 3 - Winter 1996</u>)

The Legacy of Cosmic Glue

...*what I call the download* (number 1)

Her hands are gentle, firm
Not frail, fingers of aha
wisdom, grip earned, sun burned
And as she places those warm hands upon you
hugs you to her
It is then she remembers
her child tiny just like you
And the touch from her parents, and her grandparents
In those days when she visited them
Ancestral love is in her touch, a download
Of her memory
Of her knowledge
Of her experience
To YOU
(and whether or not you are aware)
(Even if you don't remember)
That love becomes yours
Ancestor after ancestor after ancestor
Handed down... cosmic love, cosmic glue

(This download is secret and one of the most precious in this world) © *2017 published in Mental Midgets | Musqonocihte (2018) (Earth: Clipart)*

safe numbers

While the strippers bars are full of drunks,
support groups are full of lonely wives
while their children play with drugs
In an alley behind the school house
You see their faces
The pain they can't talk about,
locked up
In hurt, loss, disappointment
Secret gardens in full bloom

Out of numbness
humans hide their secrets
But the face can't lie
No one can be that careful
Each of them runs from their feelings
Because pain hurts,
because it's work to change things,
Because we're not taught how
to recover from disappointment
So we become dead out of fear

If we dare, if we dare
The reward is great,
Fear's control disappears
Your heart opens

Air suddenly flows in and out
Like you wake from a nightmare

Almost too weak to walk
You're able to see the circus,
reliving safe numbers and situations
No one but you could break the spell
When the shell breaks
You're fragile like a newborn
You can't return to your old life
Because it doesn't fit anymore

It's more than OK to be sensitive, it's essential,
it is necessary. . .

(c) 2006/2019

from the 2nd edition of SLEEPS WITH KNIVES

(Pile of words: Microsoft clipart)

NOTE: Disappointment is a big part of our world to a dangerous degree.   One doctor from the UK said in a lecture I attended that **Schizophrenia** (aka disappointment) is mislabeled as a severe psychiatric disorder with symptoms of emotional instability, detachment from reality, and withdrawal into the self and he himself had it. He said it was all disappointment! Other cultures treat a person with these symptoms as a shaman- in-training like in Russia. In 2006 when I drafted this, the poem was actually started when I was on-and-off living in Wisconsin, full of local taverns filled with lonely people. *Safe Numbers* still means a lot to me in the sense it still makes sense, to me at least. When you see the circus that is your life, then **magically** it can change. Mine changed. We can all change, once we see the controls placed on us.

I sang because of vibration, said a retired acting professor I met in New York City in 1979, as he looked at the shape of my pinky finger.

PHOTO: I am the lead singer in Automatic (vintage 80s) with Brian, Eric, Paul and Dave. Buzzy was our sound man. (Band Photo)

I do not consider myself a poet but I string together GOOD WORDS.

I think a poet is anybody who wouldn't call himself a poet.—Bob Dylan

"If you understand poetry, you understand everything." (I said this in 2018)

Whiskey Juliet Hotel:

How this happened?

I keep a small blank book in my bedroom—where I write down dreams or thoughts when I wake up or right before I sleep. It's crazy how some of my best ideas happen right before I sleep. I've dreamed book cover designs this way. Usually I draw diagrams.

And I keep a blank book in the living room on the couch where I read, crochet and watch movies. It has notes, ideas, thought bombs, song titles, movie titles, quotes, silly stuff, great movie lines, Herb-isms, all the books I want to buy and lots of other things I want to remember.

Scribbles become prose. Ideas for stories like **High Street**, a murder mystery were drafted like that. Even **Goo and Boozer**, a sci-fi short story was drafted this way... small scribbles and dialog. I'm still working on a story narrated by Skid, my BF dog: working title *Two Ethels of Tillamook*.

Herb doesn't even know how many ideas for books were born there on the couch, sitting with him. It's a mystery. But it works.

How Mental Midgets | Musqonocihte happened was in another older blank book. It had to be at least five years ago when it started, which was 2013-ish.

When I wrote **midgets** it sounded crazy. I kept the book title under wraps. Mental Midgets, what does it mean? It's absurd. It's maybe kinda funny. It's not about small people. But it is about how minds work, how memory functions, and how it seems to me, at least, our brain capacity is slowly shrinking, and our ability changes with chaos. Even our memory get smaller and smaller. Then MM became two books: TWINS!

This is a one sentence (short) book description: *This TWIN book is a collection of factoids, philosophy, quips, questions, code, quotes, photos, thought bombs, creative non-fiction, Native American history and prose. And it's short. Musqonocihte translates Blue Sky.*

What I didn't know in 02018 was I'd develop that book so FAST. I had cancer surgery. The book seemed urgent. It was urgent. Trump ignited many people in a new way. AND…the book is short as in page count but not in content! **ISBN:** 9781731074010 You are now reading BOOK 2 in a series: *It's A Miracle We Survived this Far*.

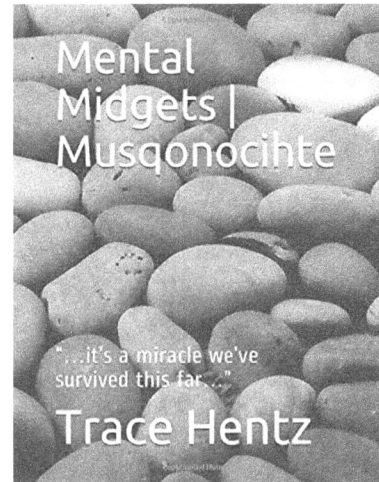

> Exposure to truth changes your life,
> period - whether that truth is a revelation
> about personal honesty and integrity
> or a divine revelation that reorganizes
> your place in the universe.
> This is why most people run from truth
> rather than toward it.
>
> Caroline Myss

I published on BEZINE in Nov. 2017

Blessed Be

Tis the season of thanks, counting our blessings and, with a new year approaching, it's time for us to take stock of what works and what doesn't.

There seems to be more wrong than right.

You know what deeply bothers me?

Indecency.

There are damaged humans in this world that hurt other people and the environment without a conscience. Whether they do it with malice or with ignorance, it still hurts humanity and our planet home. There are some among us who will destroy lives and lands for profit, and that's indecent to me. Greed is hugely indecent, and immoral.

We draft laws in America to protect us from privateers who are so greedy they can't stop themselves.

Like the oil and gas extraction companies.
Like the Big Banks, too big to fail.
Like the mining giants headed to the Arctic.
Like those ready to exterminate today's Indigenous people in the Amazon to extinction.
Like those who run for-profit industries like medical services, insurance companies, hospitals and pharmaceuticals— their callous attitude is indecent. When profit is more important than their patients, then we all should react and revolt and resist.

Today, every day, a new disaster.

"... apply Naomi Klein's concepts of the "shock doctrine" and "disaster capitalism" to it. When such disasters occur, there are always those who seek to turn a profit," wrote William Astore in 2013 for Common Dreams. "Forever war is forever profitable." Astor surmised, "War, in other words, is settled by killing, a bloody transaction that echoes the exploitative exchanges of capitalism."

All wars are banker's wars, I've blogged. Someone somewhere is making money. They might use scarcity, starvation, food insecurity, slavery, human trafficking and poverty as their weaponry. Every war is about gathering minerals or oil or water or land... whoever dies is a casualty of war, of empire. Yemen and Pine Ridge are two examples.

There is no doubt that greed poisons the mind and robs the poor. If we do not pay attention, we're utterly doomed to a repeating cycle of suffering and slavery.

In 2012 I posted on my blog an interview with brilliant Czech economist Tomas Sedlacek: Greed is the Beginning of Everything (and will kill us): (search for LARA on wordpress.) https://wp.me/p1h2Kc-PH

It's time for a revolution evolution.

Jesus started a revolution with the evolution of the heart. I always come back to his words:

From the Sermon on the Mount: (Known as the Beatitudes)

Blessed are..
...the poor in spirit: for theirs is the kingdom of heaven. (5:3)
...those who mourn: for they will be comforted. (5:4)
...the meek: for they will inherit the earth. (5:5)
...those who hunger and thirst for righteousness: for they will be satisfied. (5:6)
...the merciful: for they will be shown mercy. (5:7)
...the pure in heart: for they will see God. (5:8)
...the peacemakers: for they will be called children of God. (5:9)
...those who are persecuted for righteousness' sake: for theirs is the kingdom of heaven. (5:10)

Published: https://thebezine.com/portfolio/blessed-be/

[image: journeywithjesus.net]

Dr. Peter Beter writes:

When our Lord Jesus Christ walked the earth nearly 2000 years ago, He did many miraculous things. He healed the sick, He fed the hungry, He loved the unloved. In short, He went about doing GOOD. Most of the time our Lord astonished everyone with His patience. When He taught He found that people did not pay attention, and so He had to teach them the same lesson over and over again, and yet He never once grew angry with anyone who was seeking to learn.

Even so, He also told His disciples, "Do you think that I have come to bring peace?

No, not peace, but a sword."

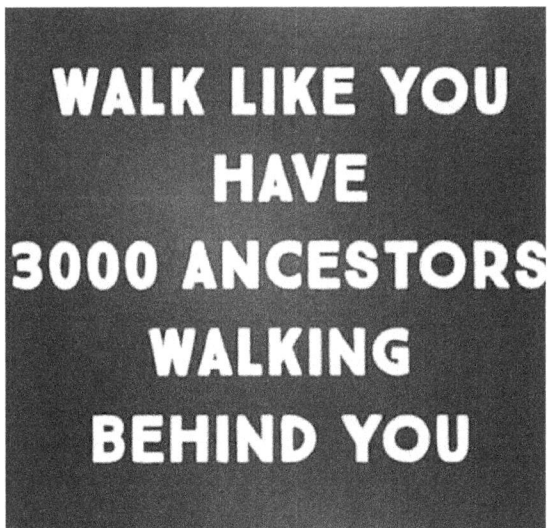

WALK LIKE YOU HAVE 3000 ANCESTORS WALKING BEHIND YOU

I read the theologian James Cone's 1970 book *A Black Theology of Liberation* in graduate school and was startled to learn that Jesus of Nazareth, the babe born in Bethlehem, was black. He came to emancipate his people from the chains of Satan, sin, and death; he then charged his followers with the same task. —MEDIUM Blogger Sam Heath

Ancestors: Pinterest Photo

WHaT JuST HaPPeNeD

My Six-Word-Story

1957: important change in human history:

Record number of sunspots=Paradigm Shift.

Race to Space? Space to what?

Pandora's Box: Manhattan Project: Killer NUKES.

End times. End Times. Bad Times.

It's (still) haves and the have-nots.

It's a club—you ain't invited.

We are creating our tomorrow today.

Bankers don't do hard-time, even busted.

Rogues and rogues-in-training = fellow future felons

P P P Psychotic Personality People

Dark Waters (2019) an anguishing watch.

Teflon Teflon Teflon: Poison Poison Poison

Am I supposed to be doing this?

Zigging Zagging will utterly confuse A.I.

My mood ring broke. OH NO!

Stay one step ahead of schedule.

Don't look back: Keep building strength.

My OCD's come back. We cool?

When will we get it right?

Empire is wide, continental, no bridges.

Bad decisions add up lots faster.

When social media murders our creativity:

Survive Create Survive Create Survive Create

Eat: Garlic, Ginger, Onions, Curcumin, Cayenne.

Call them cellphone accidents in cars.

Who would volunteer to be exterminated?

Good Monks pray day and night.

Game-show host run for president again?

Politicians dance around the hard questions.

We have learned things to overcome.

"America is still a slave plantation"

I'm saving Kentucky for a roadtrip.

Power corrupts the mind and gut.

Take a week off, little capitalists.

Rich people are still hoarding money.

Take a bow, BigOil, you won.

MY DREAM

I had a dream I was outside on a hillside, and there were many cars with many people,
people chatting, walking their dog, going to work.
But I see a wave of energy... something they didn't see.
It hits them.
Eventually it also hits them that something happened—it doesn't kill.
It transforms.

What is ~~wrong~~ with this world? What is ~~right~~ with this world? The curse is lifting.

Hard heads.
Hard lessons. © 2019

(My 2020 Photo: X marks the spot)

I eat three a day

I have never been as hungry as I am right now.
I can devour at least three chapbooks of poetry in a day when I'm **really
starving.**

Some poems are short, some chapbooks are handmade
Some poets I never heard of
but after a read and reread,
I think I know them so well I could greet them like friends.

If they are anything like me, strings of words pop in their brain, wake us up too
early.
Crossing cold floors I reach for any piece of paper I can find,
praying to myself, don't lose that.
Did I lose any? Of course.

When I was a kid, no one recommended poetry to me.
Someone should have.
I memorized Elizabeth Barrett Browning. No one made me.
Ladies Home Journal had poems. I ate them like candy.

I always start backwards when I read poetry anthologies, reading the poet's
biographies first.
The loveliest poems feel like love letters, written to me and other poets, for the
whole world,
since we're starving.
News makes hunger worse.

I don't care if they're experts, professors, laborers, waiters, stock brokers, actors,
poor farmers, high school students, priests or prostitutes, I read poets.
There are no rules.
Love every morsel and savor every tasty word they serve.

I know you know how the soul aches when you're hungry for something other
than food, or TV, when you need glimmers of light for transformation, hope, a
shimmering order of fresh familiars, "someone gets me"
because good poems churn out words like buttery gold.

I want to tell my husband a poet's soul is so open, it's too open,

Some poets are so perceptive,
    it's dangerous to watch TV.
Poets can recite drug ads word for word:
    including all the side effects: heartburn, indigestion, diarrhea, nausea,
vomiting and gas.

A Maine poet, Philip Booth, believes every poem, every work of art, everything
that is well made, well said, adds to our chances for survival... making the world
and our lives more habitable.
    He's right of course.
    Poetry teaches us to survive spiritually and literally.
Poetry hasn't killed anyone.
No one ever dies of boredom reading a chapbook. We all survive.

© 2020

(My Photo: March 2021, Sky-writings)

Where are all the little birds?

They found your body in a cornfield
They found you today (July 11)
How long had you been there?
What happened to you?
I don't know Nebraska
But I do know you.
I have your voice saved on my answering machine.
I heard the pain in your message
And I knew that pain as my own
I don't know what happened to you
You stopped breathing
Who killed you
Who killed you
Did you kill yourself?

Cynthia (Lammers) Standing Soldier (Lakota) was never able to meet her birthmother who had died in 2003. Cynthia was born in Pine Ridge and adopted out. Cynthia has died. She is another murdered missing Indigenous woman. #MMIWG (2017)
OBIT: https://kearneyhub.com/obituaries/cynthia-lammers/article_8f6d5d75-0841-5a7c-bab9-a3406f8f4661.html

Cynthia is dead. Elizabeth "Von" Hughes, also an adoptee, is dead. MaryAnn Weuke passed in 2019.
Facebook friends. Adoptees.
Beautiful lights.
Sweet souls who are now stars.
© 2021

The swarm of tourists
Throw peanuts
To the monkeys
The elites
Throw reforms and lies
To the slaves

I got me a thesaurus
For them fancy words
it hurt my head working
And I ain't likin' working
that hard on a poem
it ain't supposed to hurt
or be that much work
to love me some words

All I want to do is cross that wall
And leave this place
I'll pick vegetables, slaughter pigs, feed chickens, clean toilets, watch kids
To escape the poverty of this place
But no one told me THE MAN is on the other side of the wall too
There will always be someone waiting to exploit my labor
And rob me of a living wage and destroy a simple dream.

The bottom line was redlining
You truly cannot succeed
Since they won't let you
You cannot buy that house
In that neighborhood
No one has bootstraps for this
All I want is to cross that line out
And build community
Heal hearts
End frustration
Live well
© 2017

This This This This This This...then WHAT? (2021)

Why are we so sick?

So let me get this straight.
We can get sick from bad air, bad water, a dangerous workplace.
Don't the toxins and pollutants cause our illness?
Why are we so sick?
Are fossil fuels making us sick?
Do the Senators or Congressmen care about that?
Get out the bulldozer.
Get out more body bags.

BERNIE MEMES – I got hooked at the Biden Inaugration in 2021

Via Pinterest

HE HATED HER

He hated her so much he robbed her three times when

she was married to the millionaire. It wasn't hard. He had

their schedule and had been to their beach house many times

since she was his sister – not blood-related.

Many years he grew to hate her

Jealousy at first, but that grew into rage,

even drugs didn't help

even with her moving clear across the county,

yet he always found a way to keep her phone

number handy, yes, just in case, to keep in touch.

And she had no idea her brother wanted her dead.

His was a righteous anger

He's a born again Christian

Even after that...

it was obvious to him

Even after 30 years

She still had no clue how he really felt.

© 7-11-17

SWALLOW MANIFESTO

To our population:

We do not recognize laws, divisions, fences, borders, countries, counties, states, presidents, governors, police, park rangers, scientists, paramilitary or queens...

We are neither citizens or immigrants,

pagan or christian, wild or captive,

sinner or saint, active or inactive, atheist or evangelical,

democrat or republican, conservative or liberal, socialist or communist

American or Canadian, right wing or left wing, red state or blue state

Fettered or unfettered, safe or unsafe, foreigner or local

Sane or insane, balanced or imbalanced, pure or impure,

Insider or outsider, modest or immodest, moral or immoral.

Human labels:

misfits, holy, dangerous, judged, colonized,

controlled, saved, enslaved, damned and condemned.

Your orders:

Migrate. Fly.

My poem "Swallow Manifesto" was also published in *Tending the Fire: Native Voices and Portraits*, by Chris Felver, in 2017.

HOW DO WE HANDLE ANGER

My writer friend Gayle Meyers tells me I need to explain how we must handle anger for all the new Lost Birds (adoptees) coming after.

How do we Native people, adoptees, handle anger? We remain humble.

What do we say to the next generation? We live in our bodies but wear our hearts.

We depend on our blood roadmap, and always remain unselfish, generous.

How do we minimize the loss? We express gratitude.

How do we face hard bitter truth? We integrate and process.

We don't swallow anger. We express it.

We take in four deep breaths. We blow out four times.

We expel all the emotions then inhale fresh air.

How do we heal? We watch our children and grandkids play. We love them.

We let creativity guide us. We blog, write, sing, drum, express, represent.

We fish for salmon. We rise at dawn to pray. We are gentle with ourselves.

We regain our strength when we dream.

We see our truth and raise our vibration.

We hear the mountains.

We pray and dance in the rain.

ROCKET BODIES

Circling

Whirling

Litter

What was that?

A meteor? No.

Space Junk (aka orbital debris)

Man-made space garbage

Probably some old rocket bodies and dead satellites

thousands of pieces in pounds and tons of danger

Smaller bits: paint chips that flake away from the outsides of devices, nuts and bolts, garbage bags, a lens cap, screwdriver, and even a spatula.*

Falling faster than a speeding bullet

Waiting to hit

Anywhere

Anytime

While you're driving

When you're sleeping

HOW WHAT WHEN WHERE HOW WHY

How did this happen?

What solution? Is there a solution?

When will we hear about this on the news?

Where is the warning light?

How about a magnetic space junk garbage truck?

WHY NOT?

*2019: National Geographic: Experts predict an increasing threat of space junk that will fall to Earth.

A Forgotten Piece of Space Junk is Headed for Earth: The object could be a lost piece of a rocket dating back to the Apollo missions

A new radar system will **track** 250,000 tiny pieces of **space junk**.

from the 2nd edition of Sleeps with Knives

(Image: Rocket, Microsoft Clipart)

HOMEWORK FOR 02021

Rule #1

Raise your vibration (if it's TV or any other media or technology or a cell phone, if it feels dark to you, turn it off. NOW, please.)

Rule #2

Learn CODE (or create one)

Rule #3

Opportunity? Do you have this? Do you need this?

Then shoot me an email: tracelara@pm.me

I have one opportunity for you in Oklahoma.

Rule #4

Get involved! Are you a teacher or parent? Host a screening of the TED talk "How a Handful of Companies Control Billions of Minds Every Day" by Tristan Harris. https://humanetech.com/get-involved/ HERE

Rule #5

Force yourself? FORCE YOURSELF to feel happy—as in silly goofy crazy happy! Even if you're not—PRETEND! Give it 5 minutes each day. Do it for me and for you.

RACE

Old men jingle change in their pocket

Young people who won't even try

The trouble to be happy

Is you could look until you die

The life we have is so darn short

Busy people soon forget

An existence based on money

That's never a sure bet

I can't believe the hurry

And the race to get ahead

The harder we try to succeed

The easier we're led

What you really want to have

Won't pop up if you search

You can't start your life at the altar

When you meet your bride at the church

Our world will keep on turning

This soap opera will never die

You've got to keep on turning

'cause the next show you'll see why

The moral of this story

Is nothing will ever change

The minute you try counting

The rhythm ain't the same,

No, the rhythm ain't the same...

SO EASY

Good people.

I know good people. You know them. You are one of them.

I know and you know something is wrong in this world because we **feel** it. We may not be able to see a shape or object, but we know it's there and it's not good.

How long has this feeling been in your gut? How long? How long have you watched the movements of good people protest under attack, crunched by an invisible elite armed with propaganda and guns? How did they do it?

How? How did we forget we share one planet?

This thought came to me:

It's so easy to put a gun in your hand.

It's so easy to put an idea in your head.

Think... people... think

This is not who we are

We are not born violent

We can always stop

Watch what you watch

Say "No More" more often. We have to grow up. We must.

Think people think

Good people are individually **responsible**

... be light... shine light... be fantastically human

Your mind **is** a weapon... Keep it loaded with clarity.

Let me put an idea in your head

Love yourself first (just like they say put on your own airbag first in a jet plane)

Why? Love can be hijacked by people, fear, judgement, and the unknown. Love can be hijacked but not for long. Love yourself. No one can rob you of that.

Now go outside and tell the world how you love it... just send that thought out in your beautiful mind...

and I really do love you...

© December 2020

EVERY CELL IN YOUR BODY IS EAVESDROPPING ON YOUR THOUGHTS

(Quote Unknown Author)

YOU FEELING THIS TOO?

I wrote this wordpress post in 2015 (six years ago) but it's more accurate in 2021.

I don't know about you but I'm tired. It's dark out there.

(Yes) ... we see madmen/madwomen scurrying around everywhere, literally everywhere we look—people in panic mode and fear!

I am known as optimistic about everything. I am, actually. Even as an adoptee, even as a traumatized child, even as a journalist who has witnessed some pretty horrific stuff, even as a splitfeather with a foot in two worlds, I've never lost my hope for the future.

But I sense a foreboding darkness descending on the planet. We humans are all entering into this. I don't imagine we have to be "dark" ourselves (as in depressed) but it's hard not to notice all the upsetting news, arrests and protests, grim predictions, earth changes, as we're experiencing a tumultuous time of great unrest and change. We all have feelings and those feelings are collectively affecting the weather, the planet and the climate. We are being **traumatized** by this time period...we truly are.

Imagine if you are "down" how that can travel like a wave – and if many are feeling the same way, it can be seen as a "flow" of sadness/depression /trauma/fear, and with so many humans feeling that same "down"...this can transmit and will travel like a dark wave.

I know **and you know** that human beings are sensitive. Really sensitive! And what we perceive around us can and does actually affect us. How do we **not** experience this?

We will experience it. We cannot **not** experience trauma. We are in touch with this physical realm if we are living and breathing. (Trauma literally cracks you open...)

But but but... it hurts.... how might we avoid it? We don't. We can't. And we must not be **afraid**! (Some do believe that power thrives on collective fear. They use fear to control.)

How we can lift ourselves is truth, with humility. Speak truth to yourself, to your mate, to your kids, to your friends. Be completely truth-full. Be mind-full. Then be kind to yourself and to others!

Look around you. What's not right for you? Admit what you don't need and let it go. What can you do to make it better? Feel what you feel—but please don't bury it or deny it. See it. Feel it. Release it and let it go...

You don't have to fix the world. You only have to fix YOU! (and if you do fix you, you can change the world and that wave.)

I tell myself: Be grateful you are feeling. Be glad you are not a psychopath or narcissistic. Be glad you are able to know what is happening and this collective human trauma is necessary to break us free (as in we are birthing a new world). Whatever darkens our path doesn't need to darken us!

If I could reach through the ethers and hug you, I would. Trust me. It's gonna be alright. Eventually.

LISTEN ~~HEAR~~ LISTEN
~~HEAR~~ LISTEN ~~HEAR~~
LISTEN ~~HEAR~~ LISTEN
~~HEAR~~ LISTEN ~~HEAR~~
LISTEN ~~HEAR~~ LISTEN

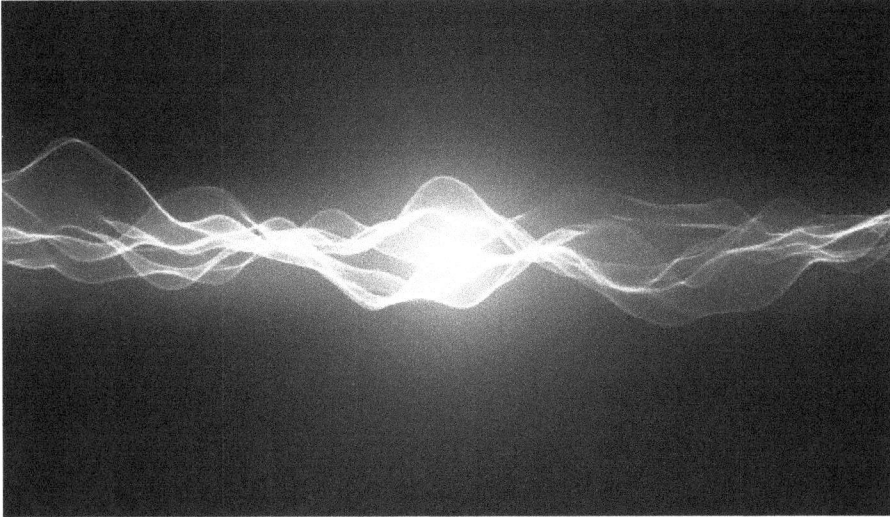

(WAVE: Microsoft clipart)

Some say our planet began the 9th Wave in 2011.

A very strong wave warning in 2020-21: There are extra energy waves coming to humanity that are empowering the manifestation of our thoughts along with everyone else's thoughts. Whatever you think about will happen much faster than normal. Whatever they think about will happen just as it does for you. So pay close attention.

[FYI: In the year 774 AD, an enormously powerful blast of matter and energy from space slammed into Earth. Nothing like it had been felt on this planet for 10,000 years (that's their theory anyway). A mix of high-energy light and hugely accelerated subatomic particles, so when this WAVE impacted Earth, it changed our atmospheric chemistry enough to be measured centuries later. Scientists think the 774 Flare may have been a special circumstance, where a powerful solar flare occurred near a streamer of gas called a filament, slamming it and accelerating the protons in it to such high energies.] https://www.syfy.com

> How we spend our days is, of course,
> how we spend our lives.
> — Annie Dillard —

"I do not so much write a book as sit up with it, as a dying friend. I hold its hand and hope it will get better." —Author Annie Dillard

The nearby farm, the pond and the horses (My 2020 Photo)

"To feel anything
deranges you. To be seen
feeling anything strips you
naked. In the grip of it
pleasure or pain doesn't
matter. You think what
will they do what new
power will they acquire if
they see me naked like
this. If they see you
feeling. You have no idea
what. It's not about them.
To be seen is the penalty."

—Author Anne Carson

An artist has got to be careful never really to arrive at a place where he thinks he's AT somewhere. You always have to realize that you're constantly in a state of becoming. And, as long as you can stay in that realm you'll sort of be alright. **—Nobel Prize Winning Musician Bob Dylan**

(Me, 1979)

A very bad break up (2021 op-ed)

Imagine you just broke up the first guy you ever loved in high school. Someone told you he was cheating on you. The more you thought about it, you grew more angry. Some of us had that experience in high school and we learned from it.

I was thinking of that older lady in Duluth, MN on TV crying because people were being so mean to Donald Trump at a rally in Duluth. I think of her even now.

Some of us had a boyfriend like Trump and we saw him for what he was—right away.

Supporters are having a bad break up with Donald Trump. He told you what to do and you did it. Sadly if you gave Trump money and believed every word he said, someone needs to sit you down and gently say, you were "taken to the bank."

Don't blame yourself please. Most of us don't see the crooks for what or who they truly are, not at first. Others see it and try to warn us but we don't want to believe there are con artists and sick people out there. We can see that disbelief in all kinds of people right now. Doctors like Mary Trump warned people online about Donald Trump's mental health disorders but not enough people paid attention.

Just like that guy in high school who didn't give you the time of day once you broke up with him: finally recognize Trump never loved you or cared about you. He never did.

This will be a very bad break up for some people.

Chalk up the past four years as a painful learning experience. (2021)

Trace DeMeyer (formerly a resident of Superior and Duluth) published in the Duluth News Tribune in 2021

BRAIN AT 3AM:

I can see you're trying to sleep, so I would like to offer you a selection of every memory, unresolved issue, or things you should have said or done today as well is in the past 40 years!

BACK AND FORTH

I keep going back and forth in my head about the absolute absurd power of governments who use social media like Facebook to track a person's comings and goings without their consent or knowledge. Think about Cambridge Analytica. Yep, I was one of their victims. They got me.

Obviously our personal lives are not private anymore. **And you might ask: why write or post or tweet or blog or write a book like this if you want privacy? Good question! I don't expect privacy.**

This constant barrage of information and things we don't want but they claim we need? No...I don't accept that. That is not something I celebrate. I quit Farcebook in 2018. (I'm barely on Twitter and Pinterest in 2021) (Graphic TV: Microsoft Clipart)

In November 2018 former Facebook president Sean Parker stated of the social media platform, "God only knows what it's doing to our children's brains."

Another top former Facebook executive Chamath Palihapitiya stated the obvious solution, "I can control my decision, which is that I don't use that shit. I can control my kids' decisions, which is that they're not allowed to use that shit."

Studies have shown that too much technology use can hamper a child's well-being. A 2014 report, published in Computers in Human Behavior, studied pre-teens who spent five days in a nature camp without access to screens. They showed improved comprehension of nonverbal, emotional cues. Too much screen time may also have negative physical effects on a child; previous research has associated TV-watching with obesity and excessive screen time with psychological difficulties.

https://www.cnbc.com/2018/06/05/how-bill-gates-mark-cuban-and-others-limit-their-kids-tech-use.html

Master or Slave

"We think we're searching Google; Google is actually searching us. We think that these companies have privacy policies; those policies are actually surveillance policies. We're told that if we have nothing to hide, then we have nothing to fear. The fact is, what they don't tell us and what we are forgetting, that if you have nothing to hide, then you are nothing, because everything about us that makes us our unique identities, that gives us our individual spirit, our personality, our sense of freedom of will, freedom of action, our sense of our right to our own futures, that's what comes from within. Those are our inner resources. That's our private realm. And it's intended to be private for a reason, because that is how it grows and flourishes and turns us into people who assert moral autonomy—an essential element of a flourishing, democratic society."

—Shoshana Zuboff, author of *Master or Slave: The Fight for the Soul of Our Information Civilization*

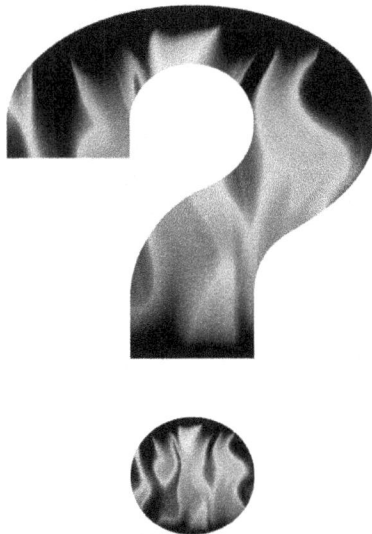

SAMI GODS (Graphic: Pinterest)

Our Grief — The War Inside Us

(July 2014 blog post) **This is not my usual post about adoption. But one thing that adoption can cause is...drum roll...SUICIDE.**

I used to think about this when I was writing my memoir —why would someone take this drastic measure?

It's obvious to me now. When guilt or grief take over your life, there is apparently no other apparent option (or few options on your list seem good enough for you to live longer and face the music for whatever you may have done or had done to you.)

If you visit a psychologist, they will talk to you and possibly drug you as an adoptee. As a joke, I posted "I AM IN BIG TROUBLE" on Facebook... It's true that Big Pharma is out to medicate you for just about everything—including: arrogance, narcissism, above-average creativity, cynicism, and antisocial behavior... (and those are just the **new** ones!)

Now I am not worried about this for me but I am worried about this for some adoptees who have not had any (emotional) support or counseling and feel isolated, sad and possibly crazy.

I'd found a statistic that adoptees do commit suicide more often than others, statistically speaking.

WHY? Unresolved (untreated) (not recognized) (buried) GRIEF!

The good news is: GRIEF IS SUBVERSIVE. It is definitely something that can be healed!

My journalist friend Suzette shared her response on FACEBOOK: In general, I find "therapy" as it currently is, as useless. I found my own method and it's a hell of a lot cheaper and you don't spend time circling and circling the same airport and never getting resolution. And guess what? You may never get resolution. But then that even becomes okay. "We're supposed to heal from grief." Is that really true? No. But you can integrate it, whatever "it" is and keep moving...

Conventional therapy has it backwards and frankly enables people to keep them emotionally broken, (in my honest opinion)..."

Growing up, I was not aware of the various medical terms for adoptee issues such as severe narcissist injury or post-traumatic stress disorder. I am sure <u>no one</u> in my family even considered I might have a problem with being adopted...

Since 2004, I read numerous studies about adoptees in treatment for "identity" issues (split feather syndrome/schizophrenia), the primal wound, reactive attachment disorder (RAD), depression and/or suicidal thoughts.

Soon I found statistics. An adoptee friend in Toronto told me to read ***Adoption: Unchartered Waters*** by Dr. David Kirschner, a book about (male) adoptees who are notorious serial killers. (I did read it.)

No, you didn't see **that** book mentioned on TV or on OPRAH or anywhere else...

No, I am not saying that adoptees have more problems than the rest of the world, <u>not at all</u>. I am saying that something big hit us emotionally hard as babies (or small children) and some of us did NOT recover—and that is something a psychologist might drug you for...

But listen to me: DRUGS are not the answer to our problems.

The war is inside us. There is a heroin and opiod epidemic where I live, and probably where you live too. WHY? People (some are even adoptees) are so desperate to numb themselves they are self-medicating.

The school shooters (like the Parkland shooter in Florida is an adoptee) were diagnosed as children with ADHD and given drugs—Ask yourself: what happens when they are older, on their own, in college—some may go stark raving mad! (Mainstream media doesn't disclose that many of the shooters were ADHD kids and medicated as young children.)

ADHD Drug Warnings:

There have been 44 warnings from eight countries (United States, United Kingdom, Canada, Japan, Australia, New Zealand, France and Singapore) warning that ADHD ***drugs/stimulants*** cause harmful side effects. These include the following (note that some warnings cite more than one side effect, so the list below may not be equal to the total number of warnings):

- 13 warnings on stimulants causing heart problems
- 10 warnings on stimulants causing mania/psychosis
- 9 warnings on stimulants causing cardiovascular problems
- 8 warnings on stimulants causing death
- 4 warnings on stimulants causing hallucinations
- 4 warnings on stimulants causing depression
- 4 warnings on stimulants causing violence, hostility or aggression
- 4 warnings on stimulants causing seizures
- 3 warnings on stimulants causing agitation or irritability
- 3 warnings on stimulants causing anxiety
- 2 warnings on stimulants causing suicide risk/attempts
- 2 warnings on stimulants causing addiction or dependence
- Read more here

So my hope is anyone reading this will consider SUICIDE as a flashing warning sign.

STOP immediately and call a suicide hotline.

If you know someone who is considering it, be their advocate and get them to make the call!

It's a SIGN you need to change your life, your direction, your path. Not take drugs but CHANGE your mind. CHANGE your thoughts—not with drugs or self-medicating behaviors—no.

If Big Pharm has its way, we'd ALL be medicated and that, my friends, is one of the scariest ideas—EVER!

Each of us has the choice. Our mental (emotional) health is **our** own problem! We all must learn to handle our emotions (with help, with support, with healing) and face the problem and GRIEVE when we need to!

UPDATE: APRIL 2021-The Food and Drug Administration (April 2) OK'd Qelbree (KELL'-bree) for treating attention deficit hyperactivity disorder in children ages 6 to 17.

"...Loving yourself is a revolutionary act..." (unknown)

"Caring for myself is not self-indulgence, it is self-preservation, and that is an act of political warfare." — Author Audre Lorde

This version of me wasn't built overnight. This is experience. This is pain. This is insecurities. This is abuse. This is depression. I had to go through things to get to the level I'm at now.

ACTIVISM:

ME ME ME ME ME ME ME ME ME ME ME ME ME
ME ME ME ME ME ME ME ME ME ME ME ME ME
ME ME ME ME ME ME ME ME ME ME ME ME ME
ME ME ME ME ME ME ME ME ME ME ME ME ME
ME ME ME ME ME ME ME ME ME ME ME ME
ME ME ME ME ME ME ME ME ME ME ME ME
ME ME ME ME ME ME ME ME ME ME ME
ME ME ME ME ME ME ME ME ME ME ME ME
ME ME ME ME ME ME ME ME ME ME ME
ME ME ME ME ME ME ME ME ME ME ME
ME ME ME ME ME ME ME ME ME ME ME ME
ME ME ME ME ME ME ME ME ME ME ME
ME ME ME ME ME ME ME ME ME ME ME
ME ME ME ME ME ME ME ME ME ME ME
ME ME ME ME ME ME ME ME ME ME ME ME
ME ME ME ME ME ME ME ME ME ME ME ME
ME ME ME ME ME WE ME ME ME ME ME ME
ME ME ME ME WE WE ME ME ME ME ME ME
ME ME ME ME ME WE WE ME ME ME ME ME
ME ME ME ME ME ME WE WE WE ME ME ME
ME ME ME ME ME WE WE WE WE WE WE WE
ME ME ME ME ME ME WE WE WE WE WE WE WE
ME ME ME ME ME ME ME WE WE WE WE WE WE WE
ME ME ME ME ME ME ME WE WE WE WE WE
ME ME ME ME ME ME ME ME WE WE WE WE WE WE
ME ME ME ME ME ME ME ME ME WE WE WE WE
ME ME ME ME ME ME ME ME ME ME WE WE
ME ME ME ME ME ME ME ME ME ME ME ME WE
ME ME ME ME ME ME ME ME ME ME ME ME

MR.FISH

//3//

M I C

:: Mike India Charlie ::

Military Industrial Complex

"Doom Scroll"

"A word after a word after a word is power..."—Author Margaret Atwood

IMAGINE, IF YOU WILL,
THE PLANET AWAKENING & EXPERIENCING
A SHIFT OF CONSCIOUSNESS SO GREAT

THAT GOVERNMENTS AROUND THE WORLD CONDUCT
PSYCHOLOGICAL WARFARE ON THEIR OWN CITIZENS IN AN
ATTEMPT TO CONTROL THEM BY LOWERING THEIR VIBRATIONS
& KEEPING THEM IN A CONSTANT STATE OF FEAR.

Top US intelligence agencies

16 or 21 spy agencies? How many bad guys can there be?

(Microsoft Clipart)

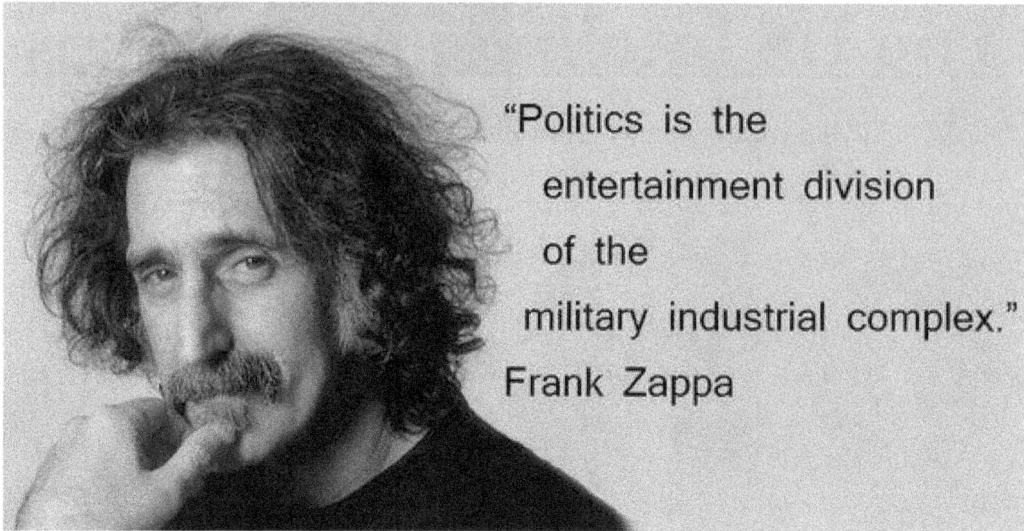

"Politics is the entertainment division of the military industrial complex."
Frank Zappa

Frank Vincent Zappa (December 21, 1940 – December 4, 1993) https://www.zappa.com

BELOW: IMAGE: https://armscontrolcenter.org/

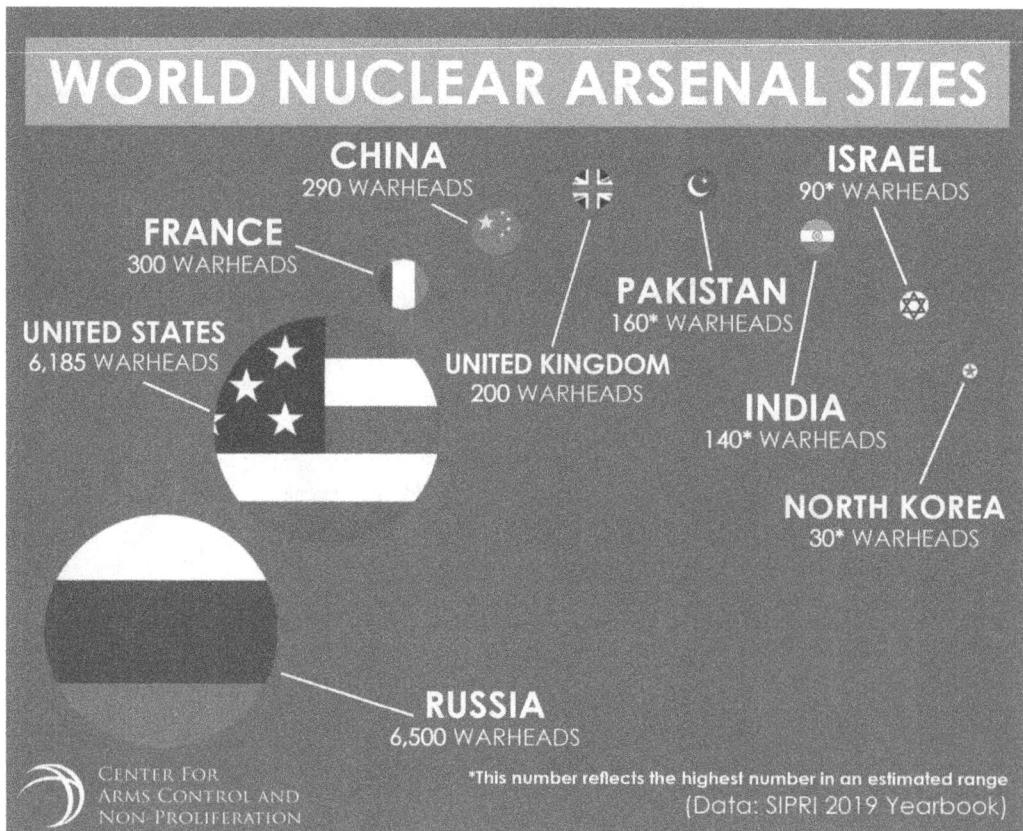

WORLD NUCLEAR ARSENAL SIZES

CHINA
290 WARHEADS

ISRAEL
90* WARHEADS

FRANCE
300 WARHEADS

PAKISTAN
160* WARHEADS

UNITED STATES
6,185 WARHEADS

UNITED KINGDOM
200 WARHEADS

INDIA
140* WARHEADS

NORTH KOREA
30* WARHEADS

RUSSIA
6,500 WARHEADS

CENTER FOR
ARMS CONTROL AND
NON-PROLIFERATION

*This number reflects the highest number in an estimated range
(Data: SIPRI 2019 Yearbook)

1957

The record number of sunspots and record-busting number of major earthquakes was a Paradigm Shift not just for the planet but for every living thing on it, as well. We as a species and our home, Planet Earth began to uncontrollably unravel and deteriorate from 1957 onwards. Ironically we were warned, at the very beginning, too. President Eisenhower famously warned the world of the ever-growing power of the military-industrial complex in his farewell speech on January 17th, 1961. It is the military-industrial complex which has gone on to develop rockets, weapons and weather warfare since Eisenhower's warning. The common denominator here was the beginning of the space race. A prominent scientist at the time, Harry Wexler who was on JFK's space team at the time warned the US government in 1962 that increased pollution from rocket exhausts was doing terrible things to the atmosphere, however, the military intervention made sure the "experiments" continued, attacking the ozone layer over your enemies country was, of course, very appealing to the military. —**Gary Walton, The Big Wobble blog** [http://www.thebigwobble.org/]

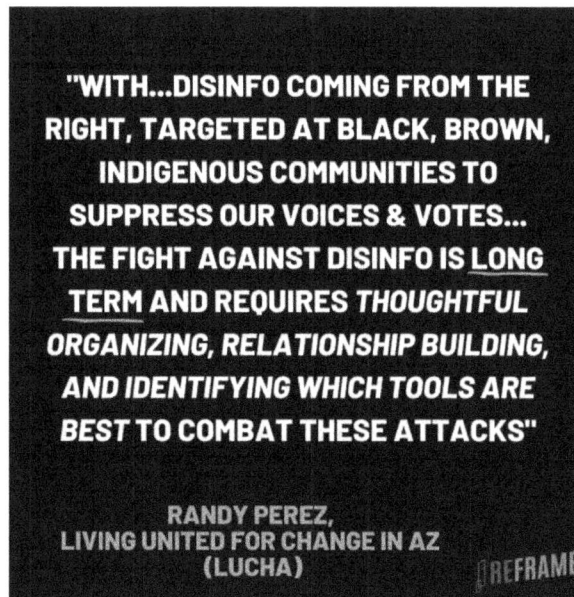

"WITH...DISINFO COMING FROM THE RIGHT, TARGETED AT BLACK, BROWN, INDIGENOUS COMMUNITIES TO SUPPRESS OUR VOICES & VOTES... THE FIGHT AGAINST DISINFO IS LONG TERM AND REQUIRES *THOUGHTFUL ORGANIZING, RELATIONSHIP BUILDING, AND IDENTIFYING WHICH TOOLS ARE BEST TO COMBAT THESE ATTACKS*"

RANDY PEREZ,
LIVING UNITED FOR CHANGE IN AZ
(LUCHA)

REFRAME

ATOMIC BOMBINGS AT 75: Scholars Speak Out Against 'Unnecessary' Attacks
August 6, 2020 by Luther Blissett

The bombing of Nagasaki as seen from the town of Koyagi, about 13 km south, taken 15 minutes after the bomb exploded. (Wikipedia)

Japan was ready to surrender, making the atomic bombings of Hiroshima on Aug. 6, 1945, and Nagasaki two days later, totally unnecessary and morally indefensible, say a panel of scholars in two video discussions. Four historians, each of whom has written extensively on the topic, discussed the documentary evidence and explored the current state of knowledge about the bombings in two sessions with TV, print, radio, and internet journalists from around the world. Among other points, they argue that the bombings were unnecessary as Japan was ready to surrender as long as they could keep the emperor (which the U.S. eventually allowed them to do); that U.S. generals, including Dwight Eisenhower and Douglas MacArthur, were opposed to the bombings; and that a real aim of the attacks was to send a message to the Soviet Union and not to avert a U.S. invasion, which was still months away.

ATOMIC COVER-UP

By Dan Kennedy | MEDIA NATION | March 29, 2021 | https://dankennedy.net/

Written and directed by the journalist Greg Mitchell, the recently released documentary "Atomic Cover-Up" is the culmination of a decades-long quest to release footage of the human suffering caused by the atomic bombs dropped on Hiroshima and Nagasaki in August 1945. Mitchell himself put years into the effort, writing a book about it in 2011 whose subtitle refers to "the greatest movie never made."

Well, now it's been made, and the terrible images captured after the bombings—including color film seen for the first time—are a testament to the lives lost and ruined. The story is told mainly by McGovern and Lt. Herbert Sussan, who died in 1985, possibly from exposure to radiation, and to whom the film is dedicated. They as well as Japanese filmmakers set about documenting the human suffering caused by the bombs only to have their work censored and suppressed.

Mitchell has brought to us a story that is both excruciating and of paramount importance. Everyone should see it. We have never come to terms with the horror of what was done in our name in August 1945. People of goodwill can differ over whether we did the right thing in order to bring a terrible war to its conclusion or if, instead, we committed unforgivable crimes against humanity.

What none of us can do is look away.

About the BOOK and FILM: https://apjjf.org/2011/9/31/Greg-Mitchell/3581/article.html

(Movie Review excerpt used with permission)

PANDORAS BOX

The Manhattan Project was a research and development undertaking during World War II that produced the first nuclear weapons. It was led by the United States with the support of the United Kingdom (which initiated the original Tube Alloys project) and Canada. From 1942 to 1946, the project was under the direction of Major General Leslie Groves of the U.S. Army Corps of Engineers. Nuclear physicist Robert Oppenheimer was the director of the Los Alamos Laboratory that designed the actual bombs. (wiki)

There was perhaps no greater proponent of information theory than John Archibald Wheeler. Wheeler was part of the Manhattan Project, and worked out the "S-Matrix" with Niels Bohr and helped Einstein develop a unified theory of physics. In his later years, he proclaimed, "Everything is information." Then he went about exploring connections between quantum mechanics and information theory. He also coined the phrase "it from bit" or that every particle in the universe emanates from the information locked inside it. At the Santa Fe Institute in 1989, Wheeler announced that everything, from particles to forces to the fabric of spacetime itself "… derives its function, its meaning, its very existence entirely … from the apparatus-elicited answers to yes-or-no questions, binary choices, bits." [https://futurism.com/john-wheelers-participatory-universe]

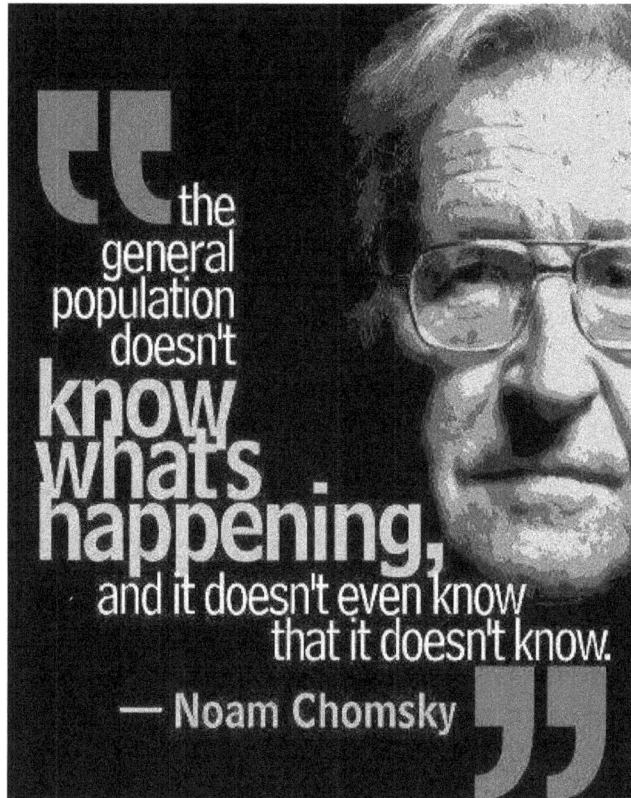

"the general population doesn't know what's happening, and it doesn't even know that it doesn't know.

— Noam Chomsky"

December 22, 1963 — exactly one month after President John F. Kennedy had been assassinated, former President Harry S. Truman published an op-ed in the *Washington Post* that most people, especially our perfumed ruling elite, wanted to ignore. Truman, who signed the CIA into existence just after World War II, wrote, "I think it has become necessary to take another look at the purpose and operations of our Central Intelligence Agency—the CIA. [...] For some time I have been disturbed by the way the CIA has been diverted from its original assignment. It has become an operational and at times a policy-making arm of the Government. This has led to trouble and may have compounded our difficulties in several explosive areas. ...There is something about the way the CIA has been functioning that is casting a shadow over our historic position and I feel that we need to correct it." Read:
https://stuartbramhall.wordpress.com/

BOMB CARBON

Until now, it has been unclear whether bomb carbon has managed to spread into the farthest crevices of the world, especially the deepest seas. It would have taken natural oceanic circulation about 1,000 years to carry it to the depths of the Mariana Trench. And in fact, testing for the new study showed that the waters of the trench did have low levels of carbon-14—which is what the researchers expected, given the long travel time from atmosphere to deep ocean. But when they used traps to catch and test crustaceans living at these depths, they detected much higher levels of the isotope in these animals' tissues and gut contents than in the surrounding waters.

The bomb carbon had to be arriving another way that brought it there faster, and the researchers surmised it was taking a shortcut via the food chain. Organic matter—including the poop and carcasses of surface-dwelling life—falls through the water column in just weeks or months. When crustaceans on the seabed munch these morsels, they absorb the signature of nuclear tests into their bodies, the researchers say in their study, published online in April 2019 in Geophysical Research Letters.
[https://agupubs.onlinelibrary.wiley.com/doi/epdf/10.1029/2018GL081514] [pdf].

Other studies conducted around the world have also recently identified the residue of the weapons tests of the mid-20th century—as well as the Chernobyl and Fukushima nuclear disasters—in mountain glaciers, another landscape often considered pristine and remote. Together with the results from the Mariana Trench, these findings "prove that atmospheric and oceanic circulation distribute bomb-derived radioactivity globally, even to the most remote sites," says Edyta Lokas of the Institute of Nuclear Physics PAS in Krakow, Poland, who worked on the glacier research, which was presented at a meeting of the European Geoscience Union (EGU) in April. Worse still, the fallout locked in glaciers includes more worrisome radioactive elements (such as americium-241, a product of the decay of plutonium)—and could be released as the world warms and the ice thaws. "The legacy of radioactive contamination will be felt by many generations ahead," Lokas says.
[https://www.scientificamerican.com/article/bomb-carbon-has-been-found-in-deep-ocean-creatures/]

Nuclear Weapons the U.S. Has Lost

Mental Floss author ERIK SASS published this on his brilliant website:

During the Cold War, the United States military misplaced at least eight nuclear weapons permanently. These are the stories of what the Department of Defense calls "broken arrows"—America's stray nukes, with a combined explosive force 2,200 times the Hiroshima bomb.

STRAY #1: Into the Pacific

February 13, 1950. An American B-36 bomber en route from Alaska to Texas during a training exercise lost power in three engines and began losing altitude. To lighten the aircraft the crew jettisoned its cargo, a 30-kiloton Mark 4 (Fat Man) nuclear bomb, into the Pacific Ocean. The conventional explosives detonated on impact, producing a flash and a shockwave. The bomb's uranium components were lost and never recovered. According to the USAF, the plutonium core wasn't present.

STRAY #2 & 3: Into Thin Air

March 10, 1956. A B-47 carrying two nuclear weapon cores from MacDill Air Force Base in Florida to an overseas airbase disappeared during a scheduled air-to-air refueling over the Mediterranean Sea. After becoming lost in a thick cloud bank at 14,500 feet, the plane was never heard from again and its wreckage, including the nuclear cores, was never found. Although the weapon type remains undisclosed, Mark 15 thermonuclear bombs (commonly carried by B-47s) would have had a combined yield of 3.4 megatons.

STRAYS #4 & 5: Somewhere in a North Carolina Swamp

January 24, 1961. A B-52 carrying two 24-megaton nuclear bombs crashed while taking off from an airbase in Goldsboro, North Carolina. One of the weapons sank in swampy farmland, and its uranium core was never found despite intensive search efforts to a depth of 50 feet. To ensure no one else could recover the weapon, the USAF bought a permanent easement requiring government permission to dig on the land.

STRAY #6: The Incident in Japan

December 5, 1965. An A-4E Skyhawk attack aircraft carrying a 1-megaton thermonuclear weapon (hydrogen bomb) rolled off the deck of the U.S.S. Ticonderoga and fell into the Pacific Ocean. The plane and weapon sank in 16,000 feet of water and were never found. 15 years later the U.S. Navy finally admitted that the accident had taken place, claiming it happened 500 miles from land in relative safety of the high seas. This turned out to be not true; it actually happened about 80 miles off Japan's Ryuku island chain, as the aircraft carrier was sailing to Yokosuka, Japan after a bombing mission over Vietnam.

These revelations caused a political uproar in Japan, which prohibits the United States from bringing nuclear weapons into its territory.

STRAYS #7 & 8: 250 kilotons of explosive power
Spring, 1968. While returning to home base in Norfolk, Virginia, the U.S.S. Scorpion, a nuclear attack submarine, mysteriously sank about 400 miles to the southwest of the Azores islands. In addition to the tragic loss of all 99 crewmembers, the Scorpion was carrying two unspecified nuclear weapons—either anti-submarine missiles or torpedoes that were tipped with nuclear warheads. These could yield up to 250 kilotons explosive power (depending which kind of weapon was used).   Publication Date: November 29, 2007 https://www.mentalfloss.com

Did you know?

The largest employer in the US is the federal government.

The US drops 46 bombs a day on average.

The USA spends $1.7 trillion on weapons.

The US has 150 hydrogen bombs (B61s) based in Europe.

World Military Expenditure grew to $1.8 Trillion in 2018.
(It was reported that the USA stopped nuclear tests in 1992. Did they?)

Number of Iraqis Slaughtered In US War And Occupation Of Iraq (War Casualties)

1,455,590

BLACK BUDGET:

Washington Examiner (2018) --Congress secretly boosted U.S. spy agency funding last year, pushing the government's intelligence "black budget" to its highest publicly known level, and raising questions about the reason for the surge.

Funding for the CIA, National Security Agency, and 14 other civilian intelligence agencies soared nearly 9 percent to $59.4 billion in fiscal 2018, and military intelligence funding grew more than 20 percent to $22.1 billion.

Overall intelligence spending increased more than 10 percent to $81.5 billion, according to figures released by the Office of the Director of National Intelligence and the Defense Department.

FOR THE COST OF THE IRAQ WAR WE COULD'VE ENDED WORLD HUNGER FOR 30 YEARS.

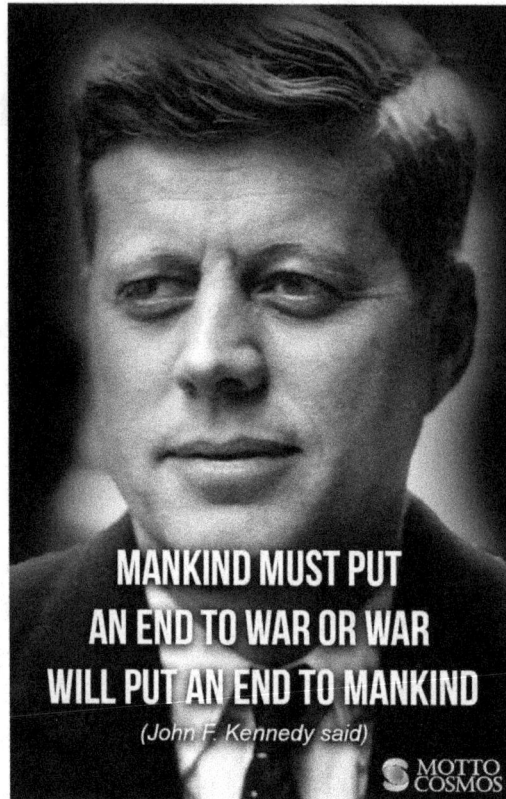

MANKIND MUST PUT
AN END TO WAR OR WAR
WILL PUT AN END TO MANKIND
(John F. Kennedy said)

MOTTO
COSMOS

(2019) The Army Quietly Re-Opens Its Infamous Germ Warfare Lab

The Fort Detrick Laboratory Experiments with Ebola, Plague and Other Deadly Toxins; Anthrax Connection

Fort Detrick was created in World War II and became the center for America's biological warfare efforts. But that role shifted in 1969, the government says, to focus solely on defense against the threat of biological weapons. In 2009, research was suspended after the discovery that more than 9,200 vials, about one-eighth of its stock, wasn't listed in the institute's database.

Research at a secretive Army germ warfare lab about 50 miles from Washington, D.C. that works with tularemia, which spreads more easily than anthrax, has been partially restarted after a federal inspection found two failures in containing unnamed germs or toxins. —SARAH OKESON, DC REPORT [HTTPS://WWW.DCREPORT.ORG/2019]

*S*ince I entered politics, I have chiefly had men's views confided to me privately. Some of the biggest men in the United States, in the field of commerce and manufacture, are afraid of something. They know that there is a power somewhere so organised, so subtle, so watchful, so interlocked, so complete, so pervasive, that they better not speak above their breath when they speak in condemnation of it.

—Woodrow Wilson, 28th President of the United States (1856-1924)

ULTRA SONIC/INFRA SONIC CANNON

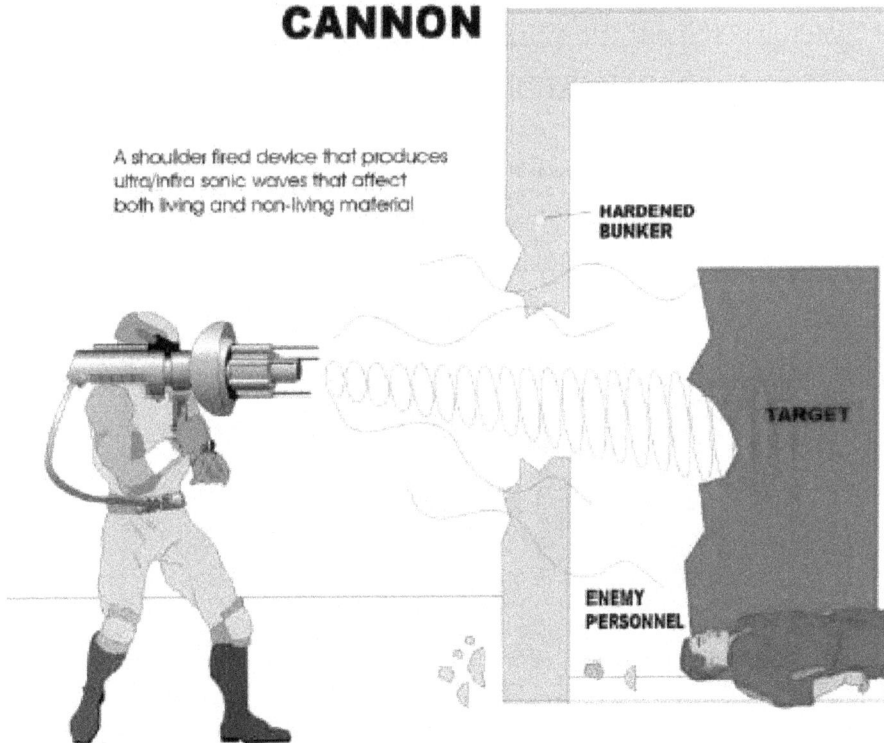

A shoulder fired device that produces ultra/infra sonic waves that affect both living and non-living material

HARDENED BUNKER

TARGET

ENEMY PERSONNEL

(Sonic Cannon GRAPHIC Microsoft Clipart)

Cost to Americans

Linear Structures Portfolio

DoD manages a reported 122,068 linear structures throughout the world, valued at approximately $185 billion. DoD's linear structures portfolio by legal interest is depicted in Table 5. The preponderance of these are utilities and ground improvements such as roads. The predominant use of DoD linear structures by PRV % is shown in Figure 4.

Service/WHS	Number of Linear Structures			
	Owned	Leased	Other	Total
Army	54,666	128	9,487	64,281
Navy	17,052	73	1,891	19,016
Air Force	30,001	39	2,224	32,264
Marine Corps	5,003	0	1,275	6,278
WHS	220	0	9	229
DoD Total	**106,942**	**240**	**14,886**	**122,068**

Table 5. DoD Linear Structure Count by Legal Interest[12]

SOURCE: https://www.quora.com/How-many-US-army-bases-are-there-in-the-world-and-how-much-is-the-cost-to-Americans

IV. Portfolio Summary

The DoD manages a worldwide real property portfolio that spans all 50 states, 8 U.S. territories with outlying areas, and 45 foreign countries. The majority of the foreign sites are located in Germany (194 sites), Japan (121 sites), and South Korea (83 sites). Locations of DoD sites by Military Service and WHS are depicted in Figure 1.

DoD Sites Distribution by Service/WHS

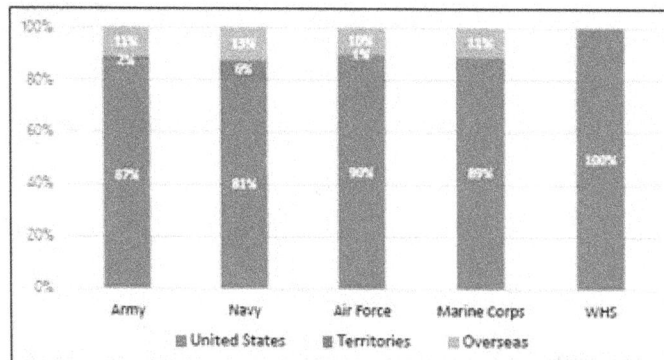

Area	Army	Navy	Air Force	Marine Corps	WHS	Total
United States	1,565	785	1,535	190	75	4,150
Territories	40	62	9	0	0	111
Overseas	202	123	166	23	0	514
DoD Total	**1,807**	**970**	**1,710**	**213**	**75**	**4,775**

Figure 1. DoD Site Count by Service/WHS

World War 2 meant many things to many people. "To over fifty million men, women, and children, it meant death. To hundreds of millions more in the occupied areas and theaters of combat, the war meant hell on earth: suffering and grief, often with little if any awareness of a cause or reason beyond the terrifying events of the moment..."—Pulitzer Prize-winning historian John Dower

Photo (right): In the 1960s, Telegraph Poles Were Equipped With Nuclear Bomb Alarms. They were simple-looking white canisters.

http://www.nationalmuseum.af.mil/shared/media/photo
db/photos/090922-F-1234S-002.jpg

The U.S. Army was in charge of exploring and mapping America. The Lewis and Clark Expedition was an all-Army affair. Army officers were the first Americans to see such landmarks as Pike's Peak and the Grand Canyon.

The U.S. Air Force was part of the Army until 1946. It was called the Army Air Corp.

Bat bombs?

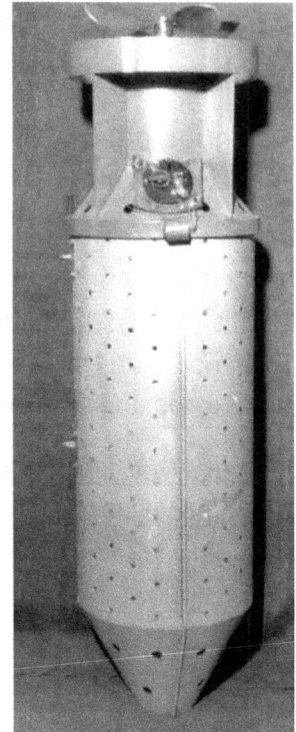

These crazy types of bombs really existed—at least they were an experimental weapon developed by the United States to attack Japan in World War II.

Hundreds of bats would be put inside each bomb-shaped case. Dropped from a bomber at dawn, the case would deploy a parachute in mid-flight and open to release the bats, each of which would have a small incendiary charge attached. The bats would then fly into houses and their tiny bombs would explode, starting fires across the wooden Japanese cities.

But for some reason (???) after an investment of about $2 million the plans for the bat bombs were shelved in 1944. (giphy.com)

Did you know?

The US has around 800 military bases in other countries, which costs an estimated $100 billion annually, a number that could be much higher depending on whether you count the bases still open in Iraq and Afghanistan.

American taxpayers are in charge of the bill for keeping these bases running.

This estimated $100 billion is pumped out of our economy to the location of these bases. It's a massive military system that ensures US influence in every corner of the planet, and given the uncontested nature of this widespread strategy, there isn't likely to be any change soon.

THE GREATEST THREAT TO PEACE:

Wealthy militarist nations like the United States think of their militaries as global police, protecting the world. The world disagrees. By a large margin people all over the world consider the United States the greatest threat to peace.

The momentum of the military-industrial complex works through the hammer-nail effect (if all you have is a hammer, every problem looks like a nail). What's needed is a combination of disarmament and investment in alternatives (diplomacy, arbitration, international law enforcement, cultural exchange, cooperation with other countries and people). Militarism has made us less safe, and continues to do so. It is not a useful tool for protection. Other tools are. Studies over the past century have found that nonviolent tools are more effective in resisting tyranny and oppression and resolving conflicts and achieving security than violence is.

Visit: WWW.WORLDBEYONDWAR.ORG

The U.S. is also by far the biggest weapons dealer, selling arms to 96 countries over the past decade, and it relentlessly invents new means of destruction. The Pentagon spent $55.9 billion on research and development last year, according to the American Association for the Advancement of Science. Compare that figure to spending on research on health ($38.9 billion), energy ($4.4 billion) and the environment ($2.8 billion). What do these numbers say about our priorities? https://www.scientificamerican.com/article/lets-defund-the-pentagon-too/

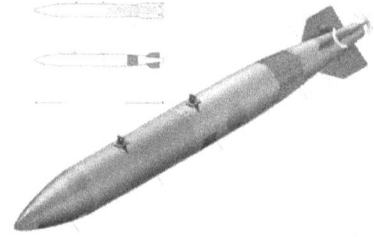

The U.S., on the other hand, has enough bases abroad to sink the world. You almost have the feeling that a single American mega-base like Bagram Air Base in Afghanistan could swallow them all up. It's so large that a special Air Force "team" has to be assigned to it just to deal with the mail arriving every day, 360,000 pounds of it in November 2010 alone. At the same base, the U.S. has just spent $130 million building "a better gas station for aircraft... [a] new refueling system, which features a pair of 1.1-million gallon tanks and two miles of pipes."

Imagine that: two miles of pipes, thousands of miles from home—and that's just to scratch the surface of Bagram's enormity. Serving 20,000 or more U.S. troops, and with the usual assortment of Burger Kings and Popeyes, the place is nothing short of a U.S. town, bustling in a way increasingly rare for actual American towns these days, part of a planetary military deployment of a sort never before seen in history. Yet, as various authors at this site have long noted, the staggering size, scope, and strangeness of all this is seldom considered, analyzed, or debated in the American mainstream. It's a given, like the sun rising in the east. And yet, what exactly is that given? As Nick Turse, who has been following American basing plans for this site over the years, points out, it's not as easy to answer that question as you might imagine. — Tom Englehardt, TOM DISPATCH http://www.tomdispatch.com/

FIRST FISSION BOMBS

FIRST FUSION BOMBS

MK IV (Fat Man), 20kt (1945)

MK-17 (Bravo), 15Mt (1955)

SINGLE WARHEAD DEVELOPMENT

MULTIPLE INDEPENDENT RE-ENTRY VEHICLE (MIRV) DEVELOPMENT

W-59, 1Mt (1962)

Minuteman I

W-87, 475kt (1986)

Peacekeeper MX

Nothing has really changed

There are obviously some serious linguistic issues and disagreements between the West and the rest of the world. Essential terms like "freedom," "democracy," "liberation," even "terrorism," are all mixed up and confused; they mean something absolutely different in New York, London, Berlin, and in the rest of the world.

Before we begin analyzing, let us recall that countries such as the United Kingdom, France, Germany and the United States, as well as other Western nations, have been spreading colonialist terror to basically all corners of the world.

And in the process, they developed effective terminology and propaganda, which has been justifying, even glorifying acts such as looting, torture, rape and genocides.

Basically, first Europe, and later North America literally "got away with everything, including mass murder."

The native people of Americas, Africa and Asia have been massacred, their voices silenced. Slaves were imported from Africa. Great Asian nations, such as China, what is now "India" and Indonesia, got occupied, divided and thoroughly plundered.

And all was done in the name of spreading religion, "liberating" people from themselves, as well as "civilizing them."

Nothing has really changed. —By Andre Vltchek, OffGuardian (used with permission)

Massive column of water rises from the ocean as an Atomic Bomb detonates at Bikini Atoll in the Pacific during the first underwater nuclear test on July 25th 1946. Read: *"Arkansas III (Battleship No. 33)"*. *Dictionary of American Naval Fighting Ships*. *Navy Department*, *Naval History and Heritage Command*.

Read about the secretive DARPA: https://en.wikipedia.org/wiki/DARPA

Copyright-free Photo: Miss Atomic Bomb poster

In this deep nest just east of Denver, the U.S. will bury some of its mighty eggs, ready for hatching

160-Foot Hole in Prairie Hides Titan Missile

Labels: PROPELLANT STORAGE / PROPELLANT MIXING PLANT / EQUIPMENT STOREHOUSE / CONTROL CENTER / ENTRANCE / ANTENNA SILO / MISSILE SILO

"HARD" MISSILE BASE may have any number of underground launching sites, or complexes. Each site contains three missile sites with auxiliary units. They are laid out as in the plan at right. A, B, and C are missile sites, with propellant and equipment terminals; D, power plant; E, control center; F, entrance; G and H, antenna sites for missile guidance at start of flight.

THE U. S. is starting to hide its deadliest weapons underground for safekeeping and constant readiness. The first buried launching sites for our longest-range ballistic missiles are now being built, 40 feet below prairie level, in eastern Colorado. On six sunken plots of earth widely dispersed around Lowry Air Force Base, workmen are constructing thermonuclear armories. Circular concrete control centers and power plants, looking like great igloos, are being erected. Holes 120 feet deep and 40 feet wide are being dug and thickly lined with con-

crete. They'll be made deeper with huge collars of concrete, 40 feet high and up to eight feet thick. Doors of steel and concrete, three feet thick, will stopper the holes, called silos.

When the launching sites are finished, they'll be completely buried. The silo doors will be level with the prairie. It will look empty and harmless again. But, underneath it, 18 Titan missiles with H-bomb warheads will stand in the silos, in perpetual firing position. They will be ready for quick, crushing retaliation in case of attack.

Other bases coming. This Colorado base is but one of 11 of the same type that the Air Force has under way. Nine more are expected to be started soon. All will be for Titans or Atlases. When the simpler, solid-fuel Minuteman is ready, perhaps two years from now, 2,600 of them will have similar holes in the ground, it is reported.

The process of constructing an underground missile base is called "hardening" it. The purpose is both to hide it and to protect it from enemy missiles. A typical hard base is depicted above.

These bases must be built as fast as possible. So Morrison-Knudsen Co., Inc., & Associates, who have the contract for the Lowry job, decided to use a "cut-and-cover" technique. This meant first sending in squadrons of bulldozers to strip off the top 40 feet of soil at each launching site. In the huge, broad trenches that resulted, the necessary structures can be built largely in the open. Further excavation, except for the missile silos, has been kept to a minimum. The silo holes have been dug by the bulldozers, snorting around in circles with 40-foot diam-

CONTINUED

96 POPULAR SCIENCE MARCH 1960

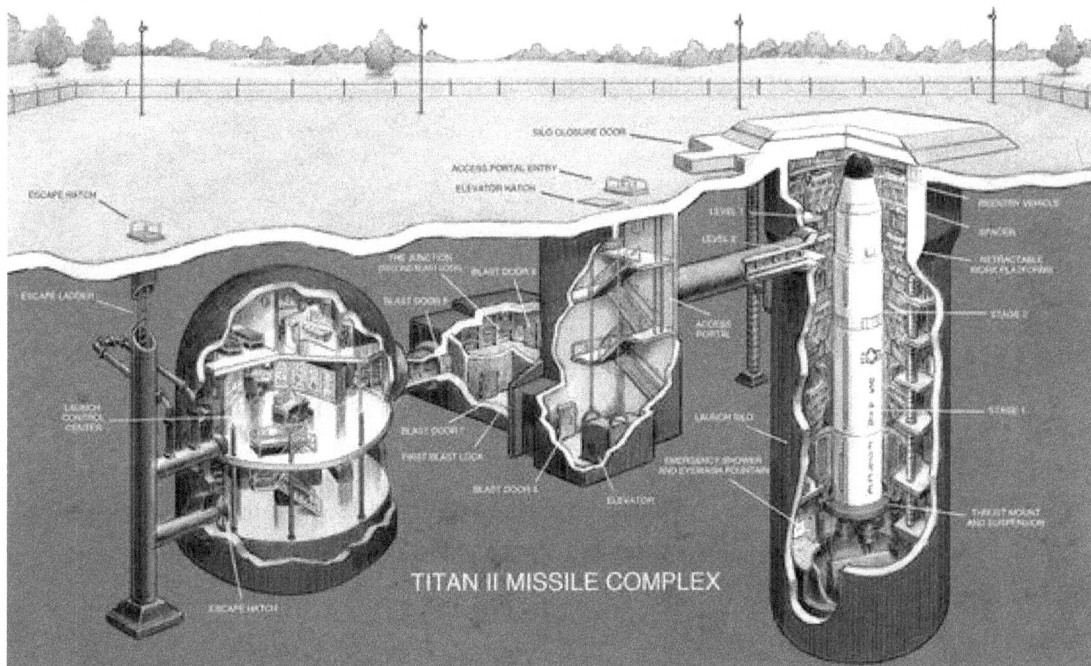

TITAN II MISSILE COMPLEX

Labels: SILO CLOSURE DOOR / ACCESS PORTAL ENTRY / ELEVATOR HATCH / ESCAPE HATCH / ESCAPE LADDER / LAUNCH CONTROL CENTER / THE JUNCTION (SECOND BLAST LOOP) / BLAST DOORS / FIRST BLAST LOCK / ESCAPE HATCH / ELEVATOR / EMERGENCY SHOWER AND EYEWASH FOUNTAIN / ACCESS PORTAL / LAUNCH SILO / LEVEL I / LEVEL II / REENTRY VEHICLE / SPACER / RETRACTABLE WORK PLATFORM / STAGE II / STAGE I / THRUST MOUNT AND SUSPENSION

MISSILE SILOS OF DAKOTA: GRAND FORKS

Nukewatch Map of the Grand Forks Air Force Base Missile Silos (1986) Photo by State Historical Society of North Dakota. This map was compiled by the anti-nuclear weapons organization, Nukewatch, in 1986. Source: SHSND 358

He had the strangest "publicity" job in history. Lt. Col. Consodine, who spent his time persuading newspapers, magazines and radio stations not to mention atoms. With one important exception, co-operation was complete.

How We Kept the Atomic Bomb Secret

By JOSEPH MARSHALL

Here's a sheaf of stories, many of them amusing, about the strange things that happened when the big hush-hush was on.

EARLY in 1945, Adolf Hitler, then at his western-front headquarters, received by courier a letter from the director of the Kaiser Wilhelm Institute, center of German atomic research. It seems probable that by this time Hitler was aware that only a near-miracle could avert total defeat and, if so, it is likely that he opened the letter with a momentary flash of hope. A successful atomic bomb, available in sufficient numbers, would have been the miracle he needed.

In the letter the director asked for more time, funds and personnel; he confessed that practical a brilliant eccentric ground to death under the wheels of the Orient Express. All the villain must do to obtain mastery of the world is to get the pa-

feet. Tickets obtained, the pair picked up the suitcase and made their way to the New York branch office of Security and Intelligence, to deliver the envelopes destined for that branch. Their horror at the discovery that the suitcase contained only Size 18 shirts and Size 42 pajamas was indescribable.

All of Capt. Dave Teeple's forces in the New York branch and Chief John O'Connell's best Police Department detectives to boot were immediately mobilized to search for the missing suitcase and a large, well-dressed man who wore Size 18 shirts and Size 42 pajamas. The two unfortunate couriers and the horrified agents of the whole Intelligence and Security Division really began to sweat.

The next day, Col. John Lansdale, the hard-

IMAGE: Photo of an article from The Saturday Evening Post article from November 1945

(2009) Northrop Grumman is hard at work on a <u>100-kilowatt laser weapon</u>, which could do far more damage, but it's not quite ready for prime time. It's fully operational, but looks like a refrigerator. Boeing announced in late December that the Avenger has been used to destroy 50 different improvised explosive devices, during tests at Redstone Arsenal in Huntsville, Alabama. — Wired Magazine writer Aaron Rowe

The maintenance and operational cost and the maintenance cost of a large size Aircraft Carrier run around $160 million per year. But wait, that is for the personnel alone! So if you add up the fuel for the aircraft and its parts for maintenance, the total operational cost for a single Aircraft Carrier per year would run around $400 million.

— https://costaide.com/aircraft-carrier-cost/

Military-grade weapons soon found their way ashore and into the hands of police. Protesters have reported LRAD attacks by police at the #NoDAPL protests at Standing Rock, during the 2017 Women's March in Washington, D.C., and in dozens of other cities and demonstrations around the world.

LRAD Sound Cannon - How Does LRAD Work | Sonic Weapon in Protests

George HW Bush Aircraft Carrier in the United States costs around $6.26 billion.

Two bunkers in Arizona once held Titan II missiles, but they are now abandoned.

The Cold War lasted 45 years, but the fear of nuclear attack peaked during the '50s and '60s. -Business Insider

NUCLEAR BUNKERS (17)

Cheyenne Mountain Complex
Construction of the Cheyenne Mountain Complex
Deep Underground Command Center
Deep Underground Support Center
Missile Master
Mount Weather Emergency Operations Center
National Audio-Visual Conservation Center
Offutt AFB nuclear bunkers
Olney Support Center
Post-Attack Command and Control System
Post-Attack Command and Control System Facility, Hadley
Project Greek Island
Raven Rock Mountain Complex
Selfridge AFB radar station
Super Combat Center
Template:US POTUS Emergency Posts
Warrenton Training Center

The Costs of War estimate shows that "from FY2003 through FY2017, the entire U.S. government directed roughly $878 billion (in nominal dollars of budget authority) to those three mission sets." Assuming that spending for the counterterrorism is roughly the same as the average spending annual spending during the FY2003-FY2017 period, this report estimates that the average annual spending for FY2018 to FY2020 is about $59 billion in current dollars. https://watson.brown.edu/costsofwar/figures

War Casualties

See (2018, March 12), "Syria War Has Killed More than 350,000 in 7 Years: Monitor," retrieved from http://www.dailymail.co.uk/wires/afp/article-5490129/Syria-war-killed-350-000-7-years-monitor.html.

In August 2018, the US acknowledged that it killed at least 1,114 civilians in the fight against ISIS in Iraq and Syria since the US intervention there in August 2014. Daragahi, Borzou (2018, September 27), "Pentagon Admits War on Isis has Killed More Than 1,100 Civilians in Syria and Iraq," The Independent, retrieved from https://www.independent.co.uk/news/world/middle-east/syria-war-isis-iraq-pentagon-civilians-killed-air-strikes-inherent-resolve-coalition-5a8558671.html

Worse, there are potentially thousands of bodies buried in rubble from bombardment in Iraq and those deaths may never be recorded. See Cockburn,Patrick (2017, July 19),"The Massacre of Mosul: 40,000 Feared Dead in Battle to Take Back City from ISIS as Scale of Civilian Casualties Revealed," Independent, retrieved from https://www.independent.co.uk/news/world/middle-east/mosul-massacre-battle-isis-iraq-city-civilian-casualties-killed-deaths-fighting-forces-islamic-state-a7848781.html

Some of the most consistent reporting of casualties caused by Coalition and Russian air strikes is at: https://airwars.org/news/coalition-civcas-jan-2018/

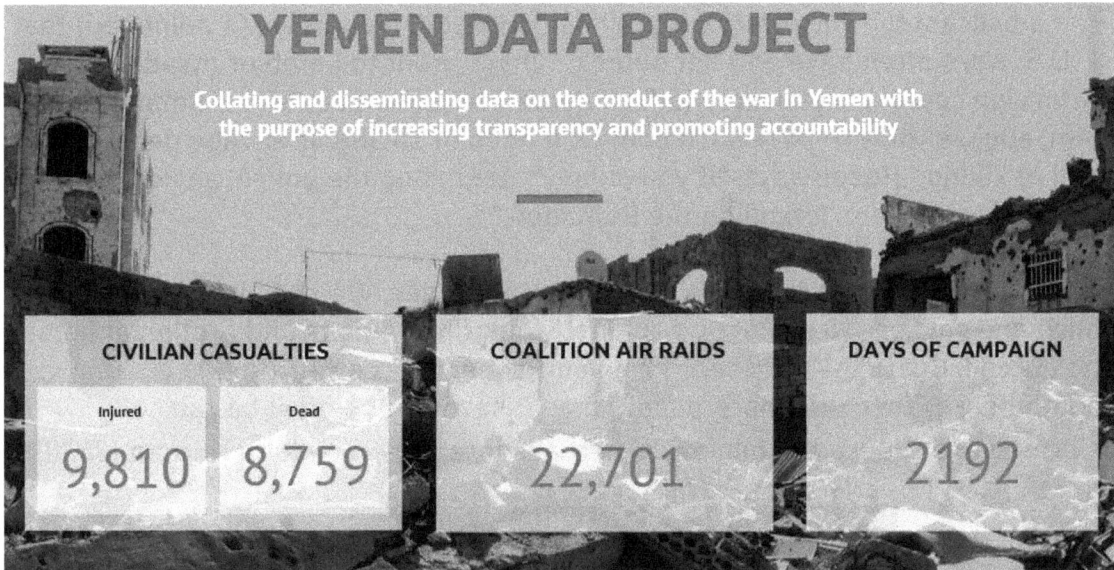

YEMEN DATA PROJECT

Collating and disseminating data on the conduct of the war in Yemen with the purpose of increasing transparency and promoting accountability

CIVILIAN CASUALTIES		COALITION AIR RAIDS	DAYS OF CAMPAIGN
Injured	Dead		
9,810	8,759	22,701	2192

The Yemen Data Project https://www.yemendataproject.org/data.html.

Neither the US or NATO have released figures on the exact number of anti-government insurgents killed. From July 1 through November 5, 2019, Afghan National Defense Forces reported killing 10,259 militants/insurgents/terrorists. https://mod.gov.af/en/press-release

See also Crawford, Neta C. (2015, May 22). "War Related Death, Injury and Displacement in Afghanistan and Pakistan 2001-2014," Costs of War, retrieved from https://watson.brown.edu/costsofwar/files/cow/imce/papers/2015/War%20Related%20Casualties%20Afghanistan%20and%20Pakistan%202001-2014%20FIN.pdf.30

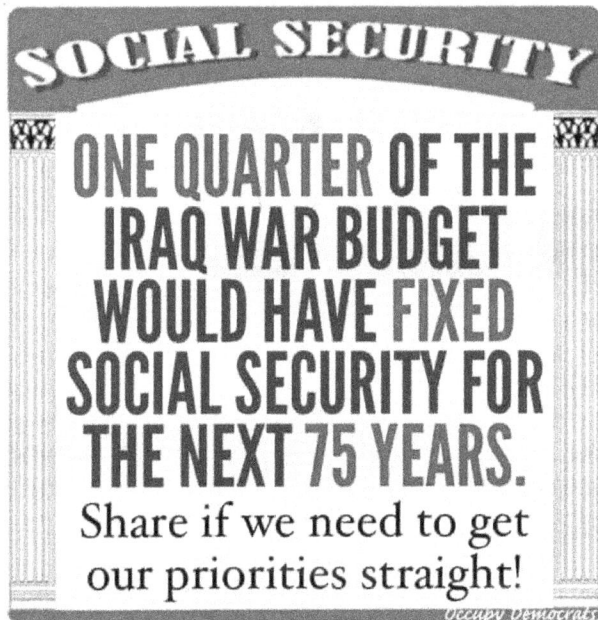

Through mid-June 2019. See Pak Institute for Peace Studies (PIPS) annual Pakistan Security Reports. Retrieved from http://pakpips.com/. https://www.satp.org/satporgtp/countries/pakistan/database/casualties.htm.

Estimating that about 9,200 Iraqi soldiers (plus or minus 1,600) were killed in 2003 resisting the US invasion and initial occupation and that about 19,000 militants were killed from 2003 to September 2007, Iraq Body Count found 20,499 "enemy" deaths in Iraq War Logs, from January 2004 through December 2009.

In a podcast for *The Intercept,* political journalist Mehdi Hasan points out that U.S. wars often have a racist subtext. "If you want to bomb or invade a foreign country … you have to first demonize those people, dehumanize them, suggest they're backward people in need of saving or savage people in need of killing," Hasan says. "If you support defunding the police, as I do, you should also support defunding the Pentagon."

I'm not advocating the total abolition of armed forces. We will always need some police and soldiers to protect us against violent individuals and groups at home and abroad. But in their present form, our armed forces resemble a chemotherapy that kills more people than it saves. They must be radically reformed and reduced to minimize their adverse effects.—John Horgan (2020)

The High Cost of Police and Prisons

In most states and localities, spending on police and prisons outweighs what the Reverend Martin Luther King Jr. once described as "programs of social uplift." The numbers are staggering. In some jurisdictions, police alone can account for up to 40 percent of local budgets, leaving little room for other priorities. In New York City, for instance, funding the police department's operations and compensation costs more than $10 billion yearly—more, that is, than the federal government spends on the Centers for Disease Control and Prevention. Nationwide, more than $100 billion annually goes into policing.

Now, add to that another figure: what it costs to hold roughly 2 million (yes 2,000,000!) Americans in prisons and jails—roughly $120 billion a year. Like policing, in other words, incarceration is big business in this country in 2020. After all, prison populations have grown by nearly 700 percent since 1972, driven in significant part by the "war on drugs," a so-called war that has disproportionately targeted people of color. —**William D. Hartung is the director of the Arms and Security Program at the Center for International Policy.**

(My 2021 Photo: Spook Moon)

How Evil Wins

This is the hidden face of a government that has no respect for the freedoms of its citizenry.

So stop with all of the excuses and the hedging and the finger-pointing and the pissing contests to see which side can out-shout, out-blame and out-spew the other. Enough already with the short- and long-term amnesia that allows political sycophants to conveniently forget the duplicity, complicity and mendacity of their own party while casting blame on everyone else.

This is how evil wins. This is how freedom falls and tyranny rises.

—By John W. Whitehead, The Rutherford Institute

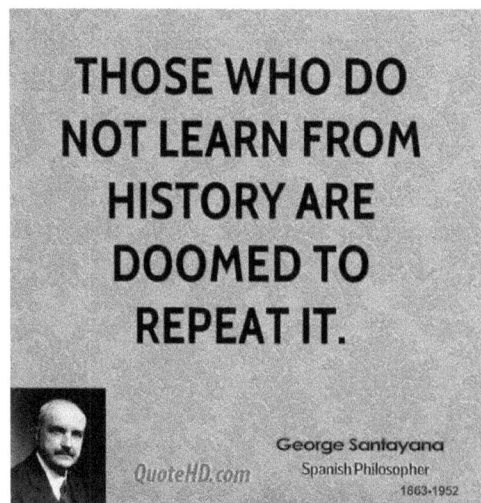

THOSE WHO DO NOT LEARN FROM HISTORY ARE DOOMED TO REPEAT IT.

George Santayana
Spanish Philosopher
1863-1952

QuoteHD.com

Our citizens should know the urgent facts...but they don't because our media serves imperial, not popular interests. They lie, deceive, connive and suppress what everyone needs to know, substituting managed news misinformation and rubbish for hard truths..."—Filmmaker **Oliver Stone**

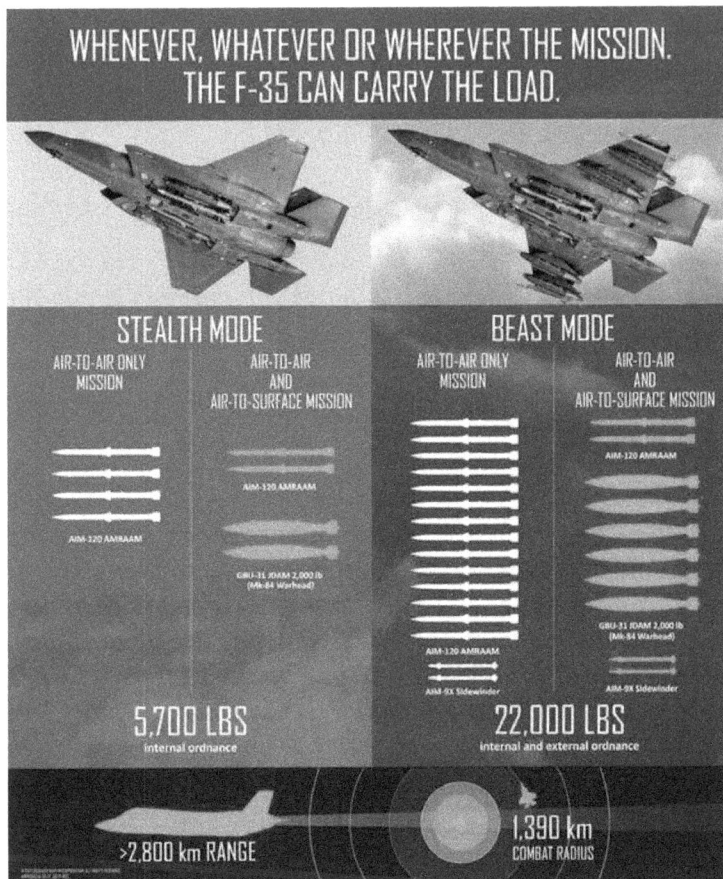

WHENEVER, WHATEVER OR WHEREVER THE MISSION. THE F-35 CAN CARRY THE LOAD.

STEALTH MODE

AIR-TO-AIR ONLY MISSION

AIR-TO-AIR AND AIR-TO-SURFACE MISSION

AIM-120 AMRAAM

AIM-120 AMRAAM

GBU-31 JDAM 2,000 lb (Mk-84 Warhead)

BEAST MODE

AIR-TO-AIR ONLY MISSION

AIR-TO-AIR AND AIR-TO-SURFACE MISSION

AIM-120 AMRAAM

AIM-120 AMRAAM

GBU-31 JDAM 2,000 lb (Mk-84 Warhead)

AIM-9X Sidewinder

AIM-9X Sidewinder

5,700 LBS
internal ordnance

22,000 LBS
internal and external ordnance

>2,800 km RANGE

1,390 km
COMBAT RADIUS

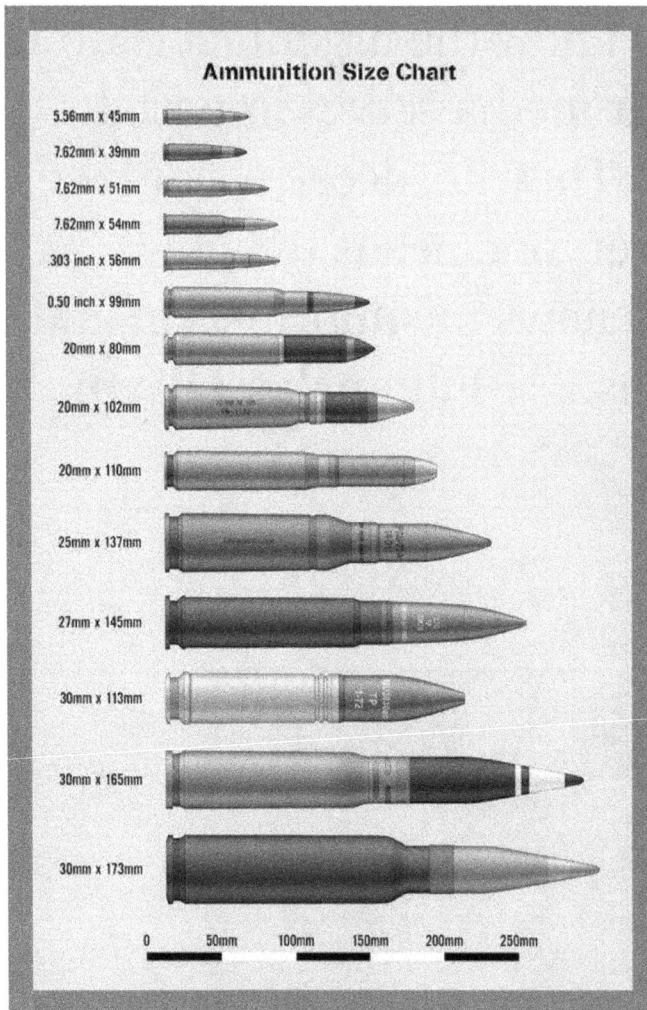

Ammunition Size Chart

Label	
5.56mm x 45mm	
7.62mm x 39mm	
7.62mm x 51mm	
7.62mm x 54mm	
.303 inch x 56mm	
0.50 inch x 99mm	
20mm x 80mm	
20mm x 102mm	
20mm x 110mm	
25mm x 137mm	
27mm x 145mm	
30mm x 113mm	
30mm x 165mm	
30mm x 173mm	

0   50mm   100mm   150mm   200mm   250mm

Sanctions

The Ambassador to the UN also noted that the United States' use of sanctions amounts to an act of war and only hurts the Venezuelan people. "*Sanctions kill, as simple as that. Sanctions are criminal sanctions, sanctions are weapons of mass destruction. You don't see the smoke, but you see the effect, you see the deleterious effect of killing and suffering,*" Moncada said. "*The sanctions use banks sanction, sanctions use ships, sanctions use insurance companies, and financial blockades. They cannot just say that they are concerned about liberty or freedom or the children in Venezuela, and then exercise a ghastly, nasty policy of calculated cruelty. They are acting like torturers, it is a collective punishment.*" —Derrick Broze, The Conscious Resistance, May 2, 2019
https://desultoryheroics.com/

Weapons Cleared (Internal & Some External):

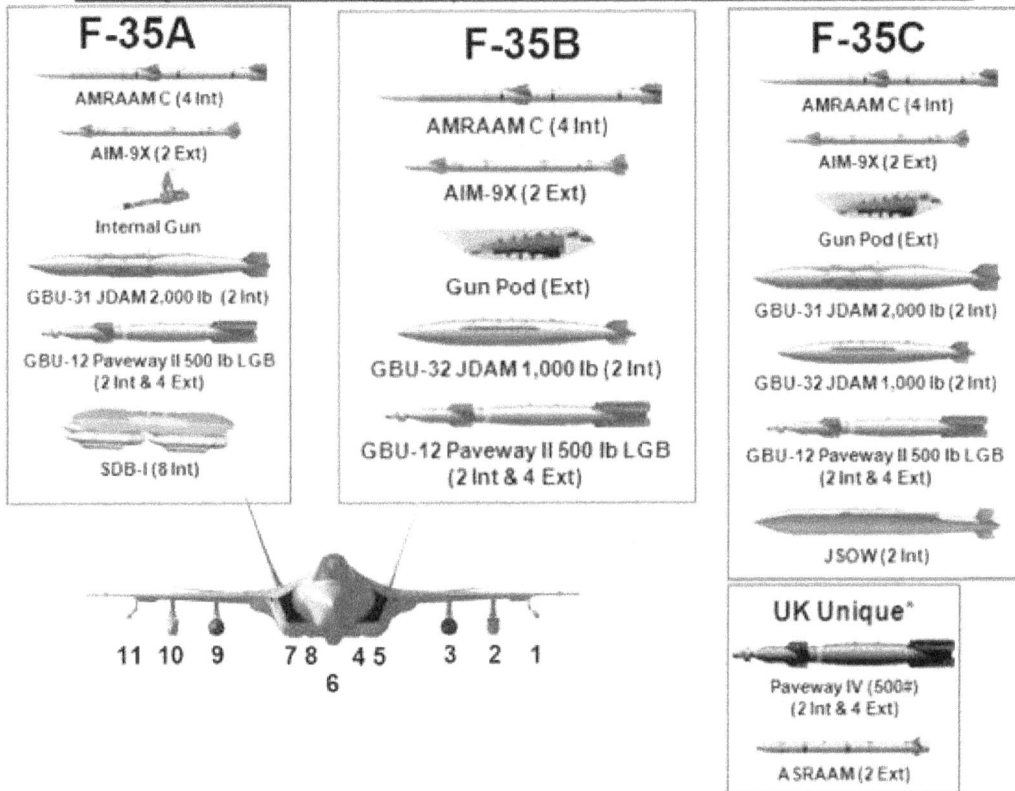

F-35A
AMRAAM C (4 Int)

AIM-9X (2 Ext)

Internal Gun

GBU-31 JDAM 2,000 lb (2 Int)

GBU-12 Paveway II 500 lb LGB
(2 Int & 4 Ext)

SDB-I (8 Int)

F-35B
AMRAAM C (4 Int)

AIM-9X (2 Ext)

Gun Pod (Ext)

GBU-32 JDAM 1,000 lb (2 Int)

GBU-12 Paveway II 500 lb LGB
(2 Int & 4 Ext)

F-35C
AMRAAM C (4 Int)

AIM-9X (2 Ext)

Gun Pod (Ext)

GBU-31 JDAM 2,000 lb (2 Int)

GBU-32 JDAM 1,000 lb (2 Int)

GBU-12 Paveway II 500 lb LGB
(2 Int & 4 Ext)

JSOW (2 Int)

UK Unique*
Paveway IV (500#)
(2 Int & 4 Ext)

ASRAAM (2 Ext)

11 10 9   7 8 4 5   3 2 1
6

The American dictatorship is by the aristocracy of the country's 585 billionaires, and has been scientifically proven beyond any doubt, now, not only in the classic Gilens and Page study, which examined thousands of bills in Congress and their money-backers and their ultimate outcomes (passage or failure to pass), during the studied period, 1981–2002. But also another (though less rigorous) study suggests that this control of the U.S. Government by America's billionaires is getting even worse. So, America is clearly a dictatorship, by America's aristocracy. —Eric Zuesse, Washington's Blog.Com

PLUTONOMY REPORT

(What middle class?)

Start with Citigroup's Plutonomy report (the report has been ruthlessly removed from the Web by Citi's lawyers)—wherein they show that, in the US, the middle class doesn't really exist. In reality, there are only two groups, a small percentage of rich households (that drive all consumption and investment) and the rest (that live hand to mouth).

The last time this happened (in the 1920s) a global depression was the inevitable result... Read: http://www.theatlantic.com/magazine/print/2011/09/can-the-middle-class-be-saved/8600/

Average Salary   (in 2011)

- Retired US Presidents .... $180,000 FOR LIFE
- House/Senate .... $174,000 FOR LIFE
- Speaker of the House .... $223,500 FOR LIFE
- Majority/Minority Leaders .... $193,400 FOR LIFE
- Teacher $40,065
- Soldier deployed in Afghanistan ... $38,000

My final thoughts?

My child is your child.

Your child is my child.

All children belong to all of us.

They all matter.

Every bomb dropped kills a child and children.

THIS matters.

THIS ends NOW. © 2021

CULTS

The Brethren

Also known as "Body of Christ" and "Garbage Eaters," the Brethren are an apocalyptic offshoot of the '70s Jesus movement, eschewing worldly possessions and earthly pleasures to purify themselves for the coming end of the world. Brethren members essentially live as vagrants, doing odd jobs to survive, eating trash, avoiding bathing and medical treatment, and giving whatever money they do make to the group.

They also forbid dancing and laughing (until the return of Jesus), bar members from communicating with family, and forbid contact between binary genders. Group founder Jim Roberts passed in December 2015, leaving the future of the secretive cult unclear.

The Seekers

The Seekers were a small sect in 1950s Chicago that firmly believed an apocalyptic flood was only months away, but that they would be whisked to safety by a flying saucer headed to another planet. As the prophesied date approached, the believers cut themselves off from society, quit their jobs, gave away their money and possessions and even extracted the metal fillings from their teeth (metal was said to prevent one from being picked up by the flying saucer).

Social psychologist Leon Festinger chronicled the cult's experience to test his now-famous theory of cognitive dissonance, later published in "When Prophecy Fails." Festinger predicted that after adherents had made these intense demonstrations of devotion, they would be all but forced to stay their course even when faced with overwhelming evidence of their leader's failed prediction.

NXIVM

Keith Raniere started NXIVM (pronounced NEX-ee-um) in 1998, positioning the group as a self-help organization with workshops and classes on empowerment. NXIVM amassed more than 18,000 followers across North America until 2017, when NXIVM members came forward exposing the abusive practices of a secret society within the group. Women were recruited under the false pretense that they were joining a sisterhood of sorts—but it ended up being a sex cult. A pyramid scheme existed within the group, with Raniere, whom members called Vanguard, at the top; "masters" who recruited other women to the secretive group; and at the bottom were the newest recruits, who were referred to as "slaves." In 2020, Raniere was tried in court, where more than a dozen women came forward with statements regarding his psychological and sexual abuse. He was convicted of many crimes, including sex trafficking, racketeering, and child pornography. Victims were as young as 15 years old. Raniere was sentenced to life in prison.

THE TRUE RUSSIAN ORTHODOX CHURCH

The True Russian Orthodox Church was an offshoot of the Russian Orthodox Church, founded by Pyotr Kuznetsov. In 2007, around 30 members of the group holed themselves up in a Russian cave, where Kuznetsov had told them to wait until the world ended in 2008 (he didn't go into the cave with them). They believed things like credit cards and barcodes were satanic and threatened to kill themselves if any authorities tried to remove them from the cave. After two members died in the cave (one from cancer, the other from starvation), some members eventually decided to leave because they were worried about toxic fumes from the corpses; others left when the cave's roof started to collapse in 2008.

One day many will hang their
heads in shame when they
realize the evil they defended
and the heroes they ridiculed.

Clipart from Microsoft was used in this section MIC.

LIFELINES

"I will not participate in the lie today..." —John Trudell

Don't trust anyone who isn't angry.

John Trudell

Lifelines: Trudell's activism and sacrifice

"When Columbus got off the boat, he asked us who we were. We said, "We're the Human Beings, we're the People." Conceptually, the Europeans didn't understand that, it was beyond their conceptual reality. They didn't see us. They couldn't see who we were. Historically, we went from being Indians to pagans to savages to hostiles to militants to activists to Native Americans. Its 500 years later and they still can't see us. We are still invisible…. They can't deal with the reality of who we are because then they'd have to deal the reality of what they have done… So they have to fear us, not recognize us, not like us… The very fact of calling us Indians creates a new identity for us, an identity than began with their arrival. Changing identity, creating a new perceptual reality, is another form of genocide. It's like severing a spiritual umbilical cord that reaches into the ancestral past. The history of the Indians begins with the arrival of Europeans. The history of the People begins with the beginning of the history of the People… The history of the People under attack is not very long, in an evolutionary context not very long, it's only 500 years. The object of civilizing us is to make Indian history become our permanent reality. The necessary objective of Native People is to outlast this attack, however long it takes, to keep our identity alive."

—John Trudell, in INDIAN COUNTRY by Gwendolen Cates, Grove Press Books, 2001

As accurate as this statement is, Santee Sioux poet activist John Trudell massively changed our ideas, our history, our narrative, by marking the invader's attack as personal, visible, and literally ongoing. Crazy Horse and Ancestors reached him so he could reach us.

But it almost didn't happen. John's family was murdered.

When Trudell's wife and family were killed in 1979, **lifelines** arrived... lines in his thoughts... lines he would cling to during what he called the dark night of the soul. Life Lines were a gift from his wife Tina, he said.

After the murders of his family, after his years in activism, after speaking out publicly for decades, on tour and in film, Trudell transformed us from defeated Indians of Hollywood westerns, in effect wiping out our extinction and stereotypes depicted in volumes of fiction.

His audiences had every skin tone. He bravely went onstage and spoke across the planet.

And they listened. We all listened.

John reached a higher power and intelligence.

He gave us prose, poems, lifelines:

"Everything that ever goes on in this dimension of reality is about energy. The thousand-year Industrial Reich evolved into the form of a Corporate Reich, emerging in the 1800s, once they found fossil fuel and ways to mine and tap this energy. The terminology changes. They created all these industrial *isms*, each for a period of time, figuring out which one served them best, which one was most efficient for their energy accumulation. The industrial ruling class now: they're still thinking this out. The Reich is built in such a way that it absorbs the energy of opposition; it feeds off the energy of the opposition. Whether civil disobedience is violent or nonviolent it is just guided in a way to absorb all that energy of opposition. To think in new terms, we need to really think with our intelligence, instead of basing our solutions on our emotional reaction."

Comparing Christopher Columbus to a virulent virus that caused an epidemic, John asked audiences, "How did my land become someone else's country?"

He addresses: in the "confined distractions of democracy," how The People still face genocidal consequences. He explains centuries of looting and theft:

The genocide of civilization is there to erase (our ancestral) memory—we don't remember we're human beings anymore. That's why there's all the false prides. That's why there's the drug use, the alcoholism. Those are symptoms of it. It's the genocide itself. It's denied itself. It's the genocide that's created these conditions. We've forgotten that we're human beings, and we're passing this diseased perception of reality amongst ourselves. We really need to look at who we are. It's not enough to say that 'I'm a traditionalist.' It's not enough to say 'I can speak the language.' It's not enough to say

*'We're all about respect.' It's not enough anymore. We have to understand **what** we're saying. We have to understand tradition, culture, sharing, love. That's the way it was a long time ago. That was our way of life.*

Diseased thoughts do spread like a virus, even among Indians.

John told anyone who would listen: "Everyone on the entire planet is a descendant of a tribe. Every human carries this memory encoded in our DNA. Our bone, flesh, and blood is made up of the metals, minerals, and liquids of the Earth. All things of the Earth are made up of the same things, just differently. That (connected) relationship is part of the spiritual understanding of life."

But John saw our connection as inconvenient in the missionary's religion.

I've been trying to figure out when religion—the word, the idea, the concept, the action—emerged in our reality. Somewhere another perception appeared, another consciousness based upon a human-form Creator and the idea of one God and his spreaders. Human beings have been turned into citizens and have been programmed to relate a moral loyalty to one of the names of God. Sometimes loyalty causes the human being to accept what's wrong. They act out of loyalty, because they've been programmed not to question. Then it's dangerous. —interview, High Times in 2003

Our intelligence is a very sacred power. Our intelligence (which is our defense) was manipulated for three thousand + years to create behavior that has resulted in a near complete genocide against the Earth.

In every speech, John found poetic precision to describe these conditions, telling us how we could dismantle and handle their oppression, if we could be clear, coherent, calm, and **see** what the conditions are and how governments use a playbook of distraction, creating fear and chaos, still going on today. He thought if we understood the "how," The People (you and I) would and could reclaim lands, dignity and sovereignty, stopping further loss. Righting the wrongs, it's first about seeing what is and what was unjust.

John said in a 2012 interview with Tamra Spivey/Lucid for Newtopia, "The war against the Natives has never stopped either, from the bullets of the cavalry and devastating poverty of the Sioux reservations, to the Native deaths caused by working and living amid the toxic effects of industrialization, this isn't a war; it's a massacre."

We deeply understand what he meant, even how we can use our intelligence. John could reach people in such a way that the American government deemed him dangerous. Of course the FBI declared AIM dangerous, too, justifying paramilitary actions against tribal "domestic terrorism." Eloquence is not welcome apparently, since John was followed and watched by the FBI since the late 1960s and early 1970s.

We know the predator
We see them feed on us
We are aware
To starve the beast
Is our destiny

(From John's poem NEVER TOO LOUDLY, in *Lines from the Mined Mind: The Words of John Trudell*)

John discoveries became our discoveries. A mining operation: that is what John called it. He didn't just mean corporations digging diamonds and ore, or oil extractions and new pipelines on our reservations. He meant mining us, mining us humans. Imagine human emotion as a power supply. We are food. We are a battery. People who become aware of this mining do not allow persecution to create strong emotions.

His words: "Protect your spirit because you are in the place where spirits get eaten." This predator needs and feeds off our human suffering. They cause it. The loss of John's family in an arson fire is an extreme example of a system that mines human emotions.

He wasn't exclusive about his warnings.

For years, John talked about how police and law enforcement is used as the security force for big corporations, allowing them to take natural resources (like oil and uranium) at the lowest possible cost to *them* but at a very high price to **us**, costing all of us, causing destruction and climate chaos—*yes,* his words were meant for *everyone* on this planet... And with the technology that exists today, the police state is using this technology to identify people. They're using it to accumulate identities. They're using it to exercise police paramilitary maneuvers. This is training for them. They will learn something from it.

Like Trudell was watched, many Native people are watched. Look at Standing Rock and the Dakota Access Pipeline (DAPL). We are too important, even now, and still enslaved in chaos not of our own making. And the worst part: we **are** the evidence of their crimes. They don't want us around as a reminder of what they did to us. They want us invisible, poor, isolated, drunk, silent. Theft and mining is happening.

(SCANNED Photo: *Lines from the Mined Mind Book*)

John said:

"Sometimes they have to kill is. They have to kill us, because they can't break our spirit. We choose the right to be who we are. We know the difference between the reality of freedom and the illusion of freedom. There is a way to live with the earth and a way not to live with the earth. We choose the way of earth…"

"I figure when we synchronize with the Creator we begin to understand how to like ourselves. Make the decision to use the power of our creative intelligence to accomplish that. That's self-healing. The whole point of western technological industrial civilization is to eliminate spiritual knowledge and turn it into religious beliefs."

Who cares for us and educates us is a traditional role. For multitudes of landless urban Indians, we had John. He made us feel we belonged. That saved

This mining process also leaves behind poison and
toxic waste
These poisons and toxics are the fears doubts and
insecurity
That affect the human beings' perceptional reality in
such a way
The human becomes separated from the being at the
expense of being
Resulting in human beings viewing life through their
fears and inabilities
Further compounded by hiding behind masks of
pride and progress
The mining process appears to have the effect of
diminishing the
Memory of being   of being human being   no longer
recognizing
Ourselves replacing our identities with the industrial
identities
Of citizen class gender race age religion victim and
whatever

How many industrial human beings have the
experience
Of feeling powerless and while having this experience
How bad can we make ourselves feel and how does
this
Feeling affect the other human beings we interact
with
The extremes these negative feelings can be taken to
Reflect the depths of the power of our intelligence
unleashed
As we incoherently and chaotically react to the
programming
Separated from any understanding that these
intensities are power

many lives. Many say John had medicine and walked the walk as Oglala Chief Crazy Horse did, with inherited traits of a leader, traditional, sacred.

I first met the warrior author, poet, actor, musician, and political activist at the Lac Courte Oreilles Honor the Earth powwow in Wisconsin. It was the summer of 1999 and I was working with Paul DeMain (Oneida/Ojibwe), the publisher of News from Indian Country (NFIC). John sat down with us and we made small talk but honestly I was nervous, unprepared to ask him anything, other than, "Can you please sign your cd, Blue Indians?" It wasn't the right time for an interview. I was editor of *Ojibwe Akiing* and the feature writer for NFIC and our newspaper covered John's activities and the American Indian Movement (AIM) all the time.

Paul founded NFIC as a national Native newspaper. I worked there from 1996-1999. The other national Native newspaper *Indian Country Today* was founded by Tim Giago (Lakota).

The "spoken word" artist said he didn't set out to be a poet or writer. After an unspeakable tragedy took the lives of his wife, Tina, their three children and Tina's mother, back in 1979, he started writing. The fire that killed them was declared an accident by the FBI who declined to investigate. To this day, Trudell believes government operatives set the blaze, "It was murder. They were murdered as an act of war."

I knew the American Indian Movement (AIM) story:

It was after the failure of the federal government to meet the demands of the protesters at Alcatraz when John Trudell joined AIM, a spokesman for The People. AIM was founded by urban Indians in July 1968 in Minneapolis and John became active at Alcatraz in 1969. The occupation of Alcatraz was a 19-month protest on the island in the San Francisco Bay. John became one of the principal voices of the occupation, broadcasting daily as Radio Free Alcatraz.

Why would the FBI compose its longest dossier about a broadcaster speaking from a rocky island a mile offshore? What was Trudell saying that frightened them so much? Trudell was advocating for Native American self-determination, explaining its moral and political importance to all Americans. On air, he often revealed the innumerable ways the government was violating Native American rights: obstructing fishing access in Washington State, setting unfair prices on tribal lands, removing Native American children from local schools. But he didn't just reveal the cruel contradictions at the heart of American society. He imagined a future in which equality—between different American cultures, and between all people and the earth itself—would become a reality. And for the first time, non–Native American communities were listening. More than 100,000 people tuned in to Pacifica stations in California, Texas and New York to hear his weekly broadcast. — https://narratively.com/native-radio-alcatraz-fbi/

On February 11, 1979, as part of a protest against the Bureau of Indian Affairs, John burned the U.S. flag outside the J. Edgar Hoover Building. "I burned the American flag as an act of protest against the injustice being extended against all of the people," he said. The next night, Tina Manning Trudell was asleep at home with their three children on the Duck Valley Indian Reservation in Nevada. She awoke to the smell of smoke and a pounding on the door. Fire filled the house. It was too late to run. Tina, who was pregnant with a boy they intended to name Josiah Hawk, perished, as did all three of their young children — Ricardo Starr, Sunshine Karma and Eli Changing Sun, and Tina's mother.

"I died then," Trudell said in the eponymous documentary about his life. "I had to die in order to get through it. And if I can get through it, then maybe I would learn how to live again." John withdrew from AIM. He sought asylum in Canada, where he struggled with shock and post-traumatic stress.

Investigations of Peltier, AIM and the murder of the two FBI agents, what became known as *The Incident at Oglala* was powerfully recounted in a film by Robert Redford, as to why Peltier was serving two life sentences and why he should be released. (I watched the movie in Seattle.)

In June 1975, two FBI agents were shot at close range and killed during a shootout at the Jumping Bull Ranch. (My Lakota friend Tony Bush took me out to see the land and the ranch.)

On the day of the shoot-out in 1975, 133,000 acres of lands that the traditional Lakotas and AIM were fighting to protect, got signed away (stolen) in Washington DC.

A family with small children was trapped in cross fire and a young Oglala warrior, Joseph Bedell Stuntz (Killsright) was killed. (His killing was never investigated. I visited his gravesite and left tobacco.)

FBI agents Coler and Williams were also dead. More than thirty Native men, women, and children were surrounded by over 150 FBI agents, SWAT, Bureau of Indian Affairs police, and local vigilantes. The family escaped despite heavy gunfire.

Three members of AIM were charged with murder. Indicted were: Darryl Butler, Robert Robideau and Leonard Peltier, who had escaped to Canada. An eyewitness testified that the three men joined the shooting after it had started. In 1991, Peltier admitted firing back at agents in an interview. Both Butler and Robideau were acquitted at trial while Peltier was tried separately and controversially convicted in 1976 and is still serving two consecutive life sentences.

In February 1998 I was in Pine Ridge to cover the 25th anniversary of the Wounded Knee 71-day Occupation in South Dakota.

Around 200 American Indians had participated in the Occupation in 1973; gunshots were frequently exchanged with the surrounding federal, state and local forces. Talks with government lawyers centered on the 27 multinational corporations invading the sacred Black Hills for oil drilling and uranium mining.

I'd interviewed Leonard Peltier by phone from his offices in Lawrence, Kansas while he was still imprisoned in Leavenworth in 1998.

Earlier in 1996 I'd interviewed Ramsey Clark who was Peltier's defense attorney and NFIC published my transcript of Clark's historic speech in Minneapolis at the Native American Journalist's conference. (I won a news writing award for that.)

John told *High Times* in 2003: "AIM, the political entity, woke people up. It added fire to a dwindling spirit. It put the fire back into life for Native people. We became more spiritually attuned to who we were. That's the most enduring fire, the most important fire. That's what I see truly as the result of the political movements."

The Great Lie is that this is civilization. It's not civilized. It has literally been the most blood-thirsty brutalizing system ever imposed upon this planet. This is not civilization, this is the Great Lie. Or if it does represent civilization, and that is truly what civilization is, then the Great Lie is that civilization is good for us.

~ John Trudell

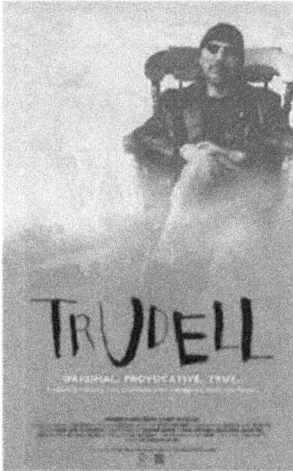

Jimmy Looks Twice, John's role in the 1992 film *Thunderheart* was based on Leonard Peltier.

ACTOR: From 1989 to 2003 John acted in seven films (listed on IMDB):

Dark Blood
Indian #2 (as John Trudell Jr.)

2005 **A Thousand Roads** (Short)
Narrator

2004 **Sawtooth**
Worm

2003 **DreamKeeper** (TV Movie)
Coyote

1998 **Smoke Signals**
Randy Peone

1996 **Extreme Measures**
Tony

1994 **On Deadly Ground**
Johnny Redfeather

1992 **Thunderheart**
Jimmy Looks Twice

1989 **Powwow Highway**
Louie Short Hair

I met and interviewed John in 2000 after his Blue Indians concert at the Pequot Museum. (I was editor of the *Pequot Times* 1999-2004.)

John was not intimidating in any way or arrogant; he was very direct, quiet and introspective, very deliberate in choosing his words. John was subtle, not flashy like some musicians, without regalia on stage and other marks of indigeneity. John did not stand out like Russell Means or other famous members of AIM, some making a living as actors in Hollywood.

Earlier I'd read that John was born February 15, 1946 in Omaha, Nebraska and was raised on the Santee Sioux reservation. John's mother grew up as Mexican in Kansas and died when he was six years old.

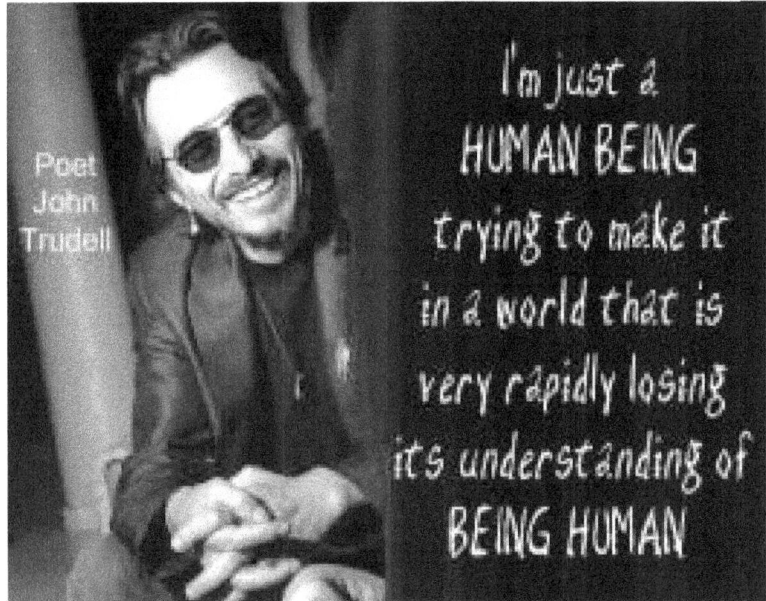

Poet John Trudell

I'm just a HUMAN BEING trying to make it in a world that is very rapidly losing its understanding of BEING HUMAN

But in 2019, I discovered in a FBI report (WFO 157-6372) that John's name is John Francis *Brown* and he was adopted by Clifford Trudell in 1946. I had no clue or I'd have asked about this part. Was it true? (I am an adoptee as well and have documented the Indian Adoption Projects in the Lost Children book series.)

In the early 1900s, Trudell's grandmother had been kidnapped by Pancho Villa's men from her tribe in Chihuahua, Mexico, and brought to the U.S. She eventually settled down in Kansas with Trudell's grandfather, a man with a price on his head for his involvement in the Mexican Revolution. A few years later, the couple had a daughter, who, after moving to Nebraska, fell in love with a Santee Sioux native, Clifford Trudell. The couple married and had John, born in a hospital close to the reservation in Omaha, on February 15, 1946. John grew up on and around the Santee reservation in North Dakota. Life felt wholesome; the reservation offered respite from the civil commotion and disarray that characterized U.S. cities, while providing sources of ritual and community. But those rather innocent early years ended abruptly at the age of 6, when Trudell's mother died in childbirth. -
https://narratively.com/native-radio-alcatraz-fbi/

Scan of page from FBI file (next)

WFO 157-6372

Subject stated he was born 2/15/46, at Omaha, Nebraska, and his file shows his birth certificate in the name JOHN FRANCIS BROWN was seen by passport authorities. File contains Affidavit dated 7/15/74, signed by [ ] and [ ] who gave their address as [ ] California. This Affidavit reads:

b6
b7C

> "We, the undersigned, knew JOHN FRANCIS BROWN when he was born in Omaha, Nebraska 15 February, 1946, to RICARDA BROWN, [ ] We also knew JOHN FRANCIS BROWN when he was subsequently adopted by CLIFFORD TRUDELL in U.S.A. 1946. Furthermore we also knew that JOHN FRANCIS BROWN was subsequently and thereinafter known as JOHN FRANCIS TRUDELL."

Subject gave his permanent residence as Box 117 Owyhee, Nevada 89832, and requested his passport be mailed in care of Inca, Incorporated, 1500 Pacific Avenue, Venice, California. He gave his home telephone number as (702) 757-3278 and his business number as (213) 392-5761. A notation on subject's application shows his passport was mailed to his home address 9/5/74.

Subject did not identify his father on his passport application. He listed his mother as RICARDA BROWN (deceased), born at Ingles, Kansas, in 1927, a U.S. citizen. He said he was last married 12/5/71, to MARUREEN T. MANNING TRUDELL who was born at Owyhee, Nevada, on 1/18/50, a citizen of the U.S., marriage not terminated, and requested she be notified in the event of accident or death at Box 117, Owyhee, Nevada 89832.

Subject was described as 5'7", brown hair, brown eyes, and tattoo on left hand. His occupation was shown as writer and his Social Security Number as 507-56-9115. Identifying document(s) submitted shown as:

> "USNR IO (Non-PO) 689-63-25 (JOHN FRANCIS TRUDELL)
> Card 1817602 iss 6-2-67
> Sel Serv 4-129-46-422 iss. 6-29-67 (JOHN FRANCIS TRUDELL)"

Photograph of JOHN FRANCIS TRUDELL, from passport file is enclosed for Minneapolis.

- 2 -

"Our power will come back to us, our sense of balance will come back to us when we go back to the natural way of protecting and honouring the Earth. If we have forgotten how to do it, and if we think that it's overwhelming and we can never accomplish, then all we have to do, each of us as an individual, is to go and find one spot on the Earth that we can relate to. Feel that energy, feel that power. That's where our safety will come. The Earth will take care of us.

We have to understand that the American Corporate State will not take care of us. They do not care about us. Maximize their profit, that is where their whole life's value is placed upon, maximize the profit. They will turn us against each other to maximize the profit, because they have done it in the past."
-John Trudell

When I wrote up my notes, I thought long and hard about using the word "prophet" to describe John, yet the word prophet felt absolutely true and still feels true. John was delivering messages openly and consistently about "mining humans" and what it means to be human and how someone else was stealing our power **and was still taking** lands. He repeated it often: **Protect your spirit.**

In the 2000 interview, an unexpected question came out of me about "prayer" and his answer was concise, directly to the point.

The takeaway: we must participate with Great Spirit when we pray, when we do ceremony.

On the Blue Indians tour, he was trying to penetrate years of programming that we'd all received in American schools and churches. His goal was to get the message to everyone, and that personally felt prophetic.

He coined the word *Blue Indians* for **all** of us who are not among the ruling elite or the 1%....

> There are no rights
> and no freedom
> without responsibility.
> I guarantee it.
>
> -John Trudell

"I called the album ***Blue Indians*** because there is a kind of spiritual and cultural genocide perpetrated on everyone that is poor in this country," Trudell said. "The advance of technology has put all of us on a kind of reservation. These are the people who can't educate their children, or afford health care. They've been robbed of life, which is what happened to Native people, so in that context, we're all Indians."

While Trudell served as National AIM Chairman from 1973-79, during that time the FBI compiled a 17,000 page file (covering Trudell's activities from 1969-80).

Of some 60 pages obtained through the Freedom of Information Act, describing Trudell as a major threat to national security, the memo said, "Extremely eloquent—therefore extremely dangerous."

Stay Alive

Looking back now, John left us many lifelines:

"When we think, we project electromagnetic energy out into the universe. Praying is active. When we pray, we're thinking. We are flowing with the universe. When we hope we're not projecting that energy anymore, because there's no thinking connected to it. We're just waiting for the world to deliver to us. When we're praying we're participating with the universe. The difference is about how the energy is used. The predator energy feeds on incoherency and chaos. It can't feed off of coherency. So predator energy feeds off of the chaos and incoherency generated from our unleashed fears. With coherency the predator energy wouldn't have that to feed off," John said in an interview with Tamra Spivey/Lucid in 2012.

"Use common sense. Like our selves. The sixth sense is the common sense. We all have it. I think that's the best way that we protect our spirit. To protect our individual spirit always comes down to can we use our intelligence clearly and coherently. Can we use our intelligence to recognize reality and not to judge it? Use the power of our intelligence to think more and believe less. Use the power of our creative intelligence to

"No matter what they ever do to us, we must always act for the love of our people and the earth. We must not react out of hatred against those who have no sense."
~ John Trudell

recognize reality, not to judge it, and that's how to protect our individual spirit.

"As human beings, I think we're put through a refining process which involves mining our perception of reality. Respect ourselves, our intelligence, that is how we synchronize with the Creator. It's as simple as this: be wary of people who don't like themselves."

"Our whole objective as human beings," he said, "is to stay alive... really alive. Not surviving and existing, I'm talking about alive. *Connected* to life and all living." John spoke at a 2001 event in San Francisco, held in honor of the U'wa tribe and their resistance to oil drilling on ancestral land in Colombia.

"as long as he's not bleeding he's fine
its just that
there are so damn many ways to bleed
that at times he's not really sure.....
but what the fuck
he's still standing" —**John Trudell**

(PHOTO: UK Road Sign)

John was presented with a Living Legend award at the Inaugural Native American Music Awards in 1998 which he called "Heart Medicine". Throughout the years, he appeared as a special guest participant and took the Artist of the Year award in 2000 and the Song/Single of the Year for his full length recording *Blue Indians* with Quiltman & Jackson Browne.

In 2012, Trudell became the creator of *Hempstead Project Heart* (Hemp Energies Alternative Resource Technologies), a national initiative that creates awareness of the many uses of hemp as way of establishing a green economy in America.

Then we lost John to cancer in 2015.

He told friends: "I don't want to tell people how to remember me. I want people to remember me as they remember me."

So we are to remember John as we remember him.

John Trudell
what it means to be a human being

[B]ecause ... we come from where we come from, every one of us is the descendant of a tribe. Every person in this room is a descendant of a tribe at some point in our ancestral evolution. Common, collective, genetic memory that's in there, you know, that's encoded, like I say, in the DNA.

And for every individual, encoded in our individual DNA, alright?, is the experience of our lineage from the very beginning. Whose whole perceptional reality was what I was just saying: all things have being, we're made up of the Earth — all my relations, pray to spirits. See, and they didn't pray to *man* or *human* form. The closest they came to it was they prayed to spirits that were called *ancestors*.

Alright? And because they were praying to those ancestors for help and guidance, they understood that we were borrowing today from the past *and* the future. We're borrowing it from both places.

So they had this understanding of reality. So they knew that to *keep the balance* was the purpose. That was the purpose. The reason for being was to keep the balance.

So this was like, you know, what I will call a *spiritual* perception of reality. And so because of the spiritual perception of reality they understood that life was about *responsibility*. It wasn't about the abstraction of freedom — it was about responsibility. That life was about responsibility.

—John Trudell, 15 March 2001

Rudolph Steiner, Another Prophet:

Steiner (1861-1925) wrote:

"There are beings in the spiritual realms for whom anxiety and fear emanating from human beings offer welcome food. When humans have no anxiety and fear, then these creatures starve. People not yet sufficiently convinced of this statement could understand it to be meant comparatively only. But for those who are familiar with this phenomenon, it is a reality. If fear and anxiety radiates from people and they break out in panic, then these creatures find welcome nutrition and they become more and more powerful. These beings are hostile towards humanity.

Everything that feeds on negative feelings, on anxiety, fear and superstition, despair or doubt, are in reality hostile forces in supersensible worlds, launching cruel attacks on human beings, while they are being fed. Therefore, it is above all necessary to begin with that the person who enters the spiritual world overcomes fear, feelings of helplessness, despair and anxiety. But these are exactly the feelings that belong to contemporary culture and materialism; because it estranges people from the spiritual world, it is especially suited to evoke hopelessness and fear of the unknown in people, thereby calling up the above mentioned hostile forces against them."

Negative emotions are food for inimical spirits.

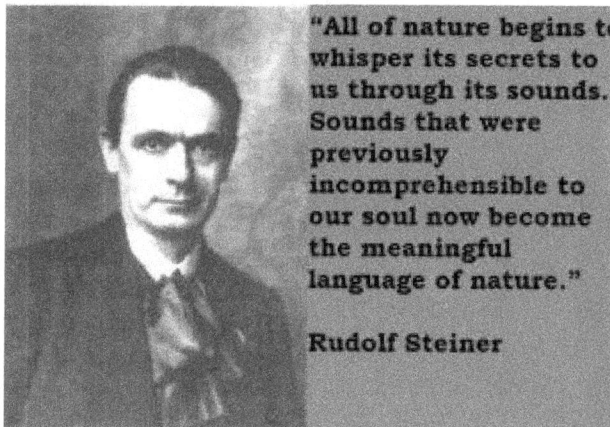

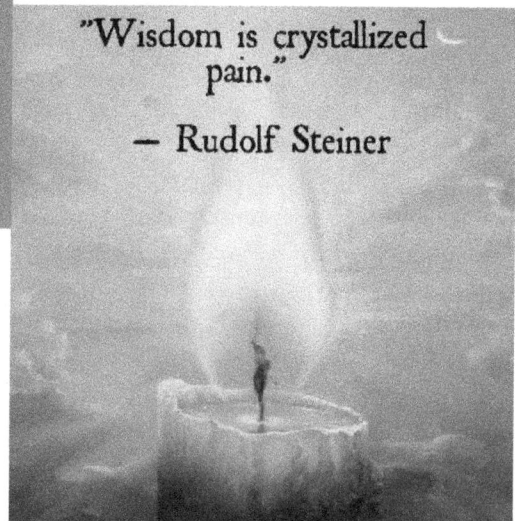

"All of nature begins to whisper its secrets to us through its sounds. Sounds that were previously incomprehensible to our soul now become the meaningful language of nature."

Rudolf Steiner

"Wisdom is crystallized pain."

— Rudolf Steiner

"ELIMINATE THE SOUL WITH MEDICINE"

theorgonizedearth More than a hundred years ago, Rudolf Steiner wrote the following:

"In the future, we will eliminate the soul with medicine. Under the pretext of a 'healthy point of view', there will be a vaccine by which the human body will be treated as soon as possible directly at birth, so that the human being cannot develop the thought of the existence of soul and Spirit.

To materialistic doctors, will be entrusted the task of removing the soul of humanity. As today, people are vaccinated against this disease or that disease, so in the future, children will be vaccinated with a substance that can be produced precisely in such a way that people, thanks to this vaccination, will be immune to being subjected to the "madness" of spiritual life.

He would be extremely smart, but he would not develop a conscience, and that is the true goal of some materialistic circles.

With such a vaccine, you can easily make the etheric body loose in the physical body.

Once the etheric body is detached, the relationship between the universe and the etheric body would become extremely unstable, and man would become an automaton, for the physical body of man must be polished on this Earth by spiritual will.

So, the vaccine becomes a kind of arymanique force; man can no longer get rid of a given materialistic feeling. He becomes materialistic of constitution and can no longer rise to the spiritual."

-Rudolf Steiner (1861-1925)

(Steiner Quotes/Images: copyright free and available online)

THE PEOPLE

The great spiritual Teachers who walked the Earth and taught the basics of the truths of the Whirling Rainbow Prophecy will return and walk amongst us once more, sharing their power and understanding with all. We will learn how to see and hear in a sacred manner. Men and women will be equals in the way Creator intended them to be; all children will be safe anywhere they want to go. Elders will be respected and valued for their contributions to life. Their wisdom will be sought out. The whole Human race will be called **The People** and there will be no more war, sickness or hunger forever.
Navajo-Hopi Prophecy of the Whirling Rainbow

Elder Dan Pine said:

"We come from the stars. They came and dropped us off here a long time ago. Even some of the animals come from there. Soon, the star people are coming back and we are gunna get our land back. Everything will go back to how it was before. Our relatives are gunna come and help us."

(My Screenshot: History Channel)

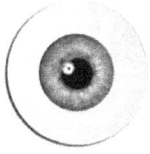

There is another, very real pandemic that is out of control: a pandemic of radiation. A pandemic that does cause kidney and heart damage and strokes, in addition to pneumonia. The radiation is produced by cell phones. The cell phones with which mothers are irradiating their babies, and joggers are irradiating their hearts. The cell phones with which 7 billion people are irradiating the birds, insects and flowers around them. The radiation that will kill all 7 billion of us, unless we put an end to it. Calling 911 will not save the Earth. Throwing away your cell phone just might. It might begin the healing. **—Arthur Firstenberg, Author,** *The Invisible Rainbow*

Scientists recently identified the oldest material on Earth: stardust that's 7 billion years old, tucked away in a massive, rocky meteorite that struck our planet half a century ago.

(My Photo 2021 Snow Moon)

PREMONITION OF A POSSIBILITY

Let us trust hope. Authentic hope is not a distraction from reality, it is the premonition of a possibility. It is time to take a stand for a transition more profound than can be encompassed in carbon metrics. What kind of change is required to know ecocide to be what the word implies—murder?

A forest is not just a collection of living trees—it is itself alive. The soil is not just a medium in which life grows; the soil is alive. So is a river, a reef, and a sea. Just as it is a lot easier to degrade, to exploit, and to kill a person when one sees the victim as less than human, so too it is easier to kill Earth's beings when we see them as unliving and unconscious already. The clearcuts, the strip mines, the drained swamps, the oil spills, and so on are inevitable when we see Earth as a dead thing, insensate, an instrumental pile of resources.

Our stories are powerful.

If we see the world as dead, we will kill it.

And if we see the world as alive, we will learn how to serve its healing.

—*Charles Eisenstein, __Extinction and the Revolution of Love__*

WHAT FUTURE DO YOU WANT?
Give to #TeamHuman

BAN KILLER ROBOTS

Ways to help:

- **Share** the call for a ban with followers, friends, family, and colleagues
- **Tag** @bankillerrobots on Twitter and tell us why you're #TeamHuman!

If you live in a region that is part of the US-centralized power alliance, everything you encounter in life will also be inextricably intertwined with the lifeblood of EMPIRE. Your money, your goods, your fuel, your way of life. It is a mess. It's a big, violent, destructive, deadly, oppressive, exploitative, omnicidal, ecocidal mess. And we're all part of it. We're all one with it. And that's really the most positive and truthful way we can look at this: yes, it's a mess, but it's not like any of us are really separate from it. At least we're in the mess together. We're all weird naked monkey mutants constructed from the fibers of murder. The most self-righteous among us is just a self-righteous murder monkey. The most wicked among us is just a wicked murder monkey. The saddest loser among us is just a failed murder monkey. - Caitlin Johnstone

ABOUT THE AUTHOR

Trace Lara Hentz (made an honorary member of the Talligewi Sovereign Nation) is an award winning journalist.

"My education began at a kitchen table in Porcupine, South Dakota on the Oglala Lakota Oyate (rez) in the early 1990s. Thanks to my relative Winyan Wa Sacha Ohmanisa (Strong Walking Woman) Ellowyn Locke (Oglala Lakota); her classroom changed my world forever," she wrote in her memoir.

She is a multi-genre author, journalist and activist. Her work is heavily focused on Native Americans and Native American adoption issues. [www.blog.tracehentz.com]

Hentz (formerly DeMeyer) has contributed writing to *Last Real Indians* and *Dissident Voice*.

She launched the publishing collective Blue Hand Books in 2011, to pay it forward, and assist other Native authors to publish their works. [www.bluehandbooks.org].

WIKI BIO: https://en.wikipedia.org/wiki/**Trace_DeMeyer**

The author lives at the foot of the Berkshire Mountains on Pocumtuckland in Greenfield Massachusetts with her fisherman/bowler husband, a retired college administrator, Herb Hentz.

I remind myself: We must understand that we are not the books we read or the jobs we get. We are more, yet somehow this truth is being lost in today's world. We are more than a grade, or a title, or a salary. We are more than a wardrobe or haircut. We are more important than any technology that will ever exist. We are a soul in progress. And each of us has to think more, be more and do more.

Thanks

I thank Anecia Tretikoff for being my sister friend collaborator and copyeditor on *What Just Happened. Her book cover photo is precious!*

Big thanks to artist Ted Littleford for permission to use his "Alive" artwork on page 27.

I also wish to thank Jerry Alatalo for interviewing me.

And I wish to thank Elliott Greenblott for the TV interview that aired in Vermont in February 2021.

Thanks Herb for the wisdom, love and Herb-isms.

BONUS CONTENT

An Interview with Trace Lara Hentz

By Jerry Alatalo on December 12, 2017

In Earth Matters, Interview Series, Native American, Sikh, Spirit Matters

Trace Lara Hentz, editor of the Lara Blog on WordPress, has graciously accepted an invitation to participate in the new interview series we began recently. She offers an impressive, unique voice and perspective which readers will appreciate, and adds valuable perceptual contrast to the worldview spectrum compiled from the excellent contributions by previous guest interviewees.

Thank you Trace Lara Hentz for kindly sharing your insights, found in the following words.

Question 1. What was your primary motivation for entering the world of blogging on the worldwide web—the internet?

Thank you very much for this invitation, Jerry.

In 2009, I joined the blogworld, first using Google Blogger. Experts say if you have a book, you must blog. Well good. That is great advice if you are a writer-author, but technically speaking, there are a million little things you won't know about blogging until you have blogged awhile. Take sidebars and widgets, for example. That first blog: American Indian Adoptees [https://blog.americanindianadoptees.com] has hit ¾ million reads in 2017. (Now it's a million more reads in 2021) And we're in the top 50 adoption blogs. I'd say it's because we are providing vital history, support and information to Native American and First Nations adoptees like myself. I found a niche and know my audience.

After my book (second edition) in 2011, I decided to try WordPress and I'm coming up on my 7th anniversary (January 2018) doing my Lara blog for more serious writing and sharing news. Time does fly. And I do blog experiments on blogger, just for fun. A few years ago I taught both blogger and WordPress at the local community college here in western Massachusetts, along with Social Media 101. They fit together like a glove.

Sharing is important, as well as having good solid interesting information on your blog. One thing I told my students is to blog/write once a week. More than that, you might get blogger-fatigue.

Question 2. How would you describe yourself with regard to spirituality—what were some of the most memorable transforming points across the years (books, personal contacts, mystical experiences, etc.) in the developing of your current spiritual perspective?

In my early 20s, I embarked on a spiritual quest. Being adopted, for me, meant searching for people and answers. Over many years, I worked to reconnect and find relatives. Along the way, I've had meaningful experiences in ceremony, in the sweatlodge, doing purification before the Sundance in Rosebud, South Dakota in the 1990s. I studied with a Northern Cheyenne in Seattle prior to the ceremony, and he helped me with contacting the medicine man who was running it. You need permission to attend and you need to know what to expect, what to bring, etc. One of the most important things I learned: do not pray for yourself in the sweat. It's not for me to say what I experienced, but it changed my life and improved my health. On that trip, I visited an Oglala Lakota family in Porcupine, SD, and soon became a relative (a member of their family). Sitting at Ellowyn's kitchen table, I learned so many things, historic things, significant things, huge things, not found in any book.

The 90s were very big years for me. In Seattle where I was living, I met with a Face Reader who was Sikh. And my Kinesiologist-Herbalist was also a Sikh. Both men were healers, definitely, and both started healing the broken parts of me. I chose to do co-counseling (trauma therapy) for three years, which was transformative. The goal: tell your whole life story, in your own words, without holding back. It's like an inner powder keg exploded. Since then I've studied herbal medicine and seek out holistic doctors for treatment. Even after all that personal growth, writing my memoir produced the biggest results in my mental health and outlook. The key is: "Know Thyself."

The one book I recommend to everyone is *John Fire Lame Deer Seeker of Visions*. If you feel a need to understand Indian Country traditions, and the work of medicine men, particularly the Lakota Oyate (Nation), this is the book to read.

Question 3. What is your greatest wish for readers as a consequence after reading and considering your writings?

My greatest wish is for those who read my blog is to be excited, and learn something new and unexpected. I share news from Indian Country, my perspective on being adopted, and I write and curate history and current events.

In case readers don't know, it took me five long years to write my memoir, prior to my first blog. Good Grief!

The one thing I had not fully realized with doing a memoir or biography, I needed to write in the first person and share my own story and the long search for my father. I was writing mostly Indian Country history in the book as a journalist. Then a literary agent read it and made recommendations. Writing friends told me similar. That started a major rewrite and a new process, while emotionally processing all of it. Writing can be a very healing thing, even writing on a blog, but it can also take you down a path you won't expect. In those five years, I healed more than I ever dreamt possible.

Writing my first full-length book was synchronicity, very well-timed. After my memoir came out, I've done a four-part book series on the Lost Children of the Indian Adoption Projects, narratives from adoptees in North America and the 60s Scoop in Canada. And I have contributed to other books on the topic of adoption.

I hope that readers who visit my Lara blog will be glad to read about Indian Country. What is news-worthy to me might be news-worthy to you.

For those new to this blog world, as you blog, you will change and evolve. Remember, it's your words and experience that people will want to read.

Question 4. Can you offer any advice to people having a difficult time dealing with government and media lies, especially as it pertains to so many average citizens who hold erroneous perceptions on important events and situations around the Earth?

If 2017 feels like a beginning, 2018 will be even more so. Yup, hold onto your hat!

It is very apparent in 2017, this is a surreal time for many Americans. The Hopi and many tribes predicted this time would come. It is a very important time, in that we are waking up and seeing things in a whole new light, with some shock and outrage and fear thrown in. History (his-story) happens in cycles, so we need to learn world history, so we can see events happening today in a historical sense, and that way discern the truth from the lies. If we don't discern, we are doomed to repeat until we do learn. I fully understand the constant news-cycle can be too much to handle... News might cause distress and bitter arguments among friends and family. That means we need to find new words, good words, better words, and to listen carefully.

I trained as a journalist in 1996 and took my first salaried job as an editor that year. Prior to that I freelanced and kept journals. Something I find most distressing today is so much history and world news is not taught in school, or included in history textbooks. There are huge chunks of history missing, mis-told, or told in a very biased, one-sided, colonized, misogynistic manner. Bloggers can change that, and I hope they will.

(ABOUT TRACE)

Known for her exceptional print interviews with influential Native Americans such as Leonard Peltier, John Trudell and Floyd Red Crow Westerman, Trace Lara Hentz (who legally dropped the name DeMeyer in 2014) started intensive research on adoptees in 2004. Trace is former editor of tribal newspapers the *Pequot Times* and *Ojibwe Akiing*. She has contributed to adoption anthologies: Lost Daughters, Adoption Reunion in the Age of Social Media, and Adoptionland: From Orphans to Activists.

***

Thank you again, Trace Lara Hentz. Peace.

Jerry's Blog: *https://onenessofhumanity.wordpress.com/author/jerryalatalo*

I MISS
MY
PRE-INTERNET
BRAIN

OTHER BOOKS by Trace L Hentz

One Small Sacrifice: The Memoir

Two Worlds: Lost Children of the Indian Adoption Projects

Called Home: The RoadMap

Stolen Generations

Mental Midgets | Musqonocihte (2018)

Sleeps with Knives (new edition 2019)

Becoming (new edition 2020)

Unraveling the Spreading Cloth of Time: Indigenous Thoughts concerning the Universe (with MariJo Moore)

BLUE INDIANS COLLECTIVE

NATIVE AMERICAN AUTHORS

Blue Hand Books is a non-profit collective of Native American and First Nations authors based in western Massachusetts, founded in 2011. Our Authors receive 100% of their book royalties. VISIT: www.bluehandbooks.org   Email: bluehandcollective@outlook.com

Please help us out and tell your friends and relatives about these books. Thank YOU!

There is no death
Only a change of worlds
— Chief Seattle

Publisher and poet Trace L Hentz is the editor and author of the historical best-selling book series "Lost Children of the Indian Adoption Projects."

HER EMAIL: tracelara@pm.me

WEBSITE: www.tracehentz.com

In Memory of Ahmaud Arbery, Breonna Taylor, Tamir Rice, Sandra Bland, Rayshard Brooks, Daniel Prude, Stephon Clark, Botham Jean, Philando Castille, Alton Sterling, Freddie Gray, Eric Garner, Akai Gurley, Michael Brown, Tanisha Anderson, Tony McDade and George Floyd, and so many other Black lives.

Congress passed the Death in Custody Reporting Act, which would enable and mandate police departments to report deaths. The intent was to better understand how to prevent these tragedies. But as of today, there is still no reporting system in place for this data collection, nor are there consequences for failing to report these numbers. In other words, official data on police killings still doesn't exist. –VOX

More than 1,000 unarmed people were killed due to police harm between 2013-2019 and one third were black, according to Mapping Police Violence.

Wolankeyawolotultiq {wool-an-kay-ow-lod-ool-tiqw} - "take good care of each other"

"You never change things by fighting the existing reality. To change something, build a new model that makes the existing model obsolete." — Buckminster Fuller

Create The World You Want Going Forward

(I am not kidding)

www.ingramcontent.com/pod-product-compliance
Lightning Source LLC
Chambersburg PA
CBHW081510040426

42447CB00013B/3181